100 Ways to Motivate Others, Third Edition

How Great Leaders Can Produce Insane
Results Without Driving People Crazy

By Steve Chandler and
Scott Richardson

THE CAREER PRESS, INC.
Pompton Plains, NJ

100 WAYS TO MOTIVATE OTHERS, THIRD EDITION
Cover design by Howard Grossman/ 12E Design
Printed in the U.S.A.

To order this title, please call toll-free 1-800-CAREER-1 (NJ and Canada: 201-848-0310) to order using VISA or MasterCard, or for further information on books from Career Press.

CAREER
PRESS

The Career Press, Inc.
220 West Parkway, Unit 12
Pompton Plains, NJ 07444
www.careerpress.com

Library of Congress Cataloging-in-Publication Data

Chandler, Steve, 1944-
    100 ways to motivate others : how great leaders can produce insane results without driving people crazy / by Steve Chandler and Scott Richardson. -- 3rd ed.
        p. cm.
    Includes index.
    ISBN 978-1-60163-243-2 -- ISBN 978-1-60163-555-6
        1. Employee motivation. 2. Leadership. I. Richardson, Scott, 1954- II. Title. III. Title: One hundred ways to motivate others.

HF5549.5.M63C434 2013
658.3'14--dc23
                                          2012027671

To Rodney Mercado

Acknowledgments

To the greatest motivator there ever was, Mr. Rodney Mercado, child prodigy, genius in 10 fields, and professor of music and violin at the University of Arizona.

To Chuck Coonradt, who, unlike other consultants, not only talks about how to motivate others, but has a proven system, the Game of Work, that delivers stunning results and fun to the workplace in the same breath. Chuck used the Game of Work on his own business first, and blew the lid off the results for his Positive Mental Attitude Audiotape company. Chuck realized that what he had created, the Game of Work system, was worth a fortune to companies of all sizes: It brought more financial success than even Positive Mental Attitude! Chuck has helped our own businesses succeed.

To motivator extraordinaire Steve Hardison, about whose talents we have written much, but never too much.

To Ron Fry, Gina Talucci, and Michael Pye at Career Press, for many years of wonderful service to our writing efforts.

And to the memory of Lyndon Duke (1941–2004), a magnificent teacher, motivator, and friend.

"While business is a game of numbers, real achievement is measured in infinite emotional wealths: friendship, usefulness, helping, learning, or, said another way, the one who dies with the most joys wins."
—Dale Dauten

Contents

Introduction to the Third Edition

The world of leadership has changed dramatically since the first edition of this book was written, and Scott Richardson and I have now revised and refreshed this organizational leadership guidebook to meet the times.

We have added 10 new ways to motivate others, bringing us into the modern world.

The book now includes fresh respect for the communication and rapid decision-making that the global community demands.

The importance of personal self-leadership and physical energy have been added to the solid leadership principles that made the first editions of this book so popular with leaders and managers of every kind of organization, from corporate, educational, and non-profit, to community groups and even families.

Motivating others requires a connection to people's deep desires. It's not just about loading them up with a lot of how-to information. Transformation is more important than information. Action is everything. A great motivator of others will value testing over trusting. She won't waste time getting her people to trust change or trust the system—she will work on ways to test them.

Change in the workplace and the world is exponential now. It is no longer linear, predictable change. It is more like the absolutely unexpected, shocking change described so dramatically in Nassim Nicholas Taleb's *The Black Swan*. Because of this, great motivators are now welcoming change and helping their people see *all* change as a creative opportunity.

Organizations are more vulnerable than ever to suddenly disappearing. They can become obsolete in a heartbeat. But rather than finding that frightening, one who masters motivating himself and others finds it exciting.

The new edition we have created for you addresses all these quantum shifts in organizational reality. It updates and upgrades your skills as a leader to motivate others to feel the same excitement you do about the global market and its opportunities. The 10 new ways to motivate others that we have added to this book are what work for us and our clients. They are not theory. And because they are not mere theory, we invite you to use them immediately, and see them as *tools, not rules*.

—Steve Chandler

1. Know Where Motivation Comes From

*Leadership is the art of getting someone else to do
something you want done because he wants to do it.*
—Dwight D. Eisenhower

There was a manager named Tom who came early to a seminar we were presenting on leadership. He was attired in an olive green polo shirt and white pleated slacks, ready for a day of golf. Tom walked to the front of the room and said, "Look, your session is not mandatory, so I'm not planning on attending."

"That's fine, but I wonder why you came early to this session to tell us that. There must be something that you'd like to know."

"Well, yes, there is," the manager confessed. "All I want to know is how to get my sales team to improve. How do I manage them?"

"Is that all you want to know?"

"Yes, that's it," declared the manager.

"Well, we can save you a lot of time and make sure that you get to your golf game on time."

The manager Tom leaned forward, waiting for the words of wisdom that he could extract about how to manage his people.

We told him: "You can't."

"What?"

"You can't manage anyone. So there, you can go and have a great game."

"What are you saying?" asked the manager. "I thought you give whole seminars on motivating others. What do you mean, I can't?"

"We do give whole seminars on this topic. But one of the first things we teach managers is that they can't really directly control their people. Motivation always comes from within your employee, not from you."

"So what is it you do teach?"

"We teach you how to get people to motivate *themselves.* That is the key. And you do that by managing agreements, not people. And that is what we are going to discuss this morning."

The manager put his car keys in his pocket and sat down in the first seat closest to the front of the room for the rest of the seminar.

2. Teach Self-Discipline

> Discipline is remembering what you want.
> —David Campbell, founder, Saks Fifth Avenue

The myth, which almost everyone believes, is that we *have* self-discipline. It's something in us, like a genetic gift, that we either have or we don't.

The truth is that we don't *have* self-discipline; we *use* self-discipline.

Here's another way to put it: self-discipline is like a language. Any child can learn a language. (All children do learn a language, actually.) Any 90-year-old can also learn a language. If you are 9 or 90 and you're lost in the rain in Mexico City, it works when you use some Spanish to find your way to warmth and safety. It works.

In this case, Spanish is like self-discipline. You were not born with it. But you can use it. In fact, you can use as much or as little as you wish. And the more you use, the more you can make happen.

If you were an American transferred to Mexico City to live for a year and needed to make your living there, the more Spanish you used the better it would be for you. If you had never used Spanish before, you could still use it. You could open your little English/Spanish phrases dictionary and start using it. You could ask for directions or help right out of that little dictionary! You wouldn't need to be born with anything special.

The same goes for self-discipline. Yet, most people don't believe that. Most people think they either have it or they don't. Most people think it's a character trait or a permanent aspect of their personality. That's a profound mistake. That's a mistake that can ruin a life.

Listen to how people get this so wrong: "He would be my top salesperson if he had any self-discipline at all," a company leader recently said. "But he has none."

Not true. He has as much self-discipline as anyone else does; he just hasn't chosen to use it yet. If the person you lead truly understood that self-discipline is something one *uses*, not something one *has*, then that person could use it to accomplish virtually any goal he ever set. He could use it whenever he wanted, or leave it behind whenever he wanted.

Instead, he worries. He worries about whether he's got what it takes, whether it's in him, whether his parents and guardians put it there. (Some think it's put there experientially; some think it's put there genetically. It's neither. It's never "put there" at all. It's a *tool* that anyone can use. Like a hammer. Like a dictionary.)

The good news is that it is never too late to correct that mistake in yourself and your people. It's never too late to learn the real truth. Enlightened leaders get more out of their people because they know that each person already has everything it takes to be successful. They don't buy the excuses, the apologies, the sad fatalism that most non-performers skillfully sell to their managers. They just don't buy it.

3. Tune in Before You Turn on

> Don't tell people how to do things, tell them what to
> do and let them surprise you with their results.
> —George S. Patton

You can't motivate someone who can't hear you.

If what you're saying is bouncing off their psychological armor, it makes little difference how good you are at saying it. You are not being heard. Your people have to hear you to be moved by you.

In order for someone to hear you, *she must first be heard.* It doesn't work the other way around. It doesn't work when you always go first. Because your employee must first appreciate that you are on her wavelength and understand her thinking completely.

As leadership guru Warren Bennis has said:

The first rule in any kind of coaching is that the coach has to engage in deep listening. Which means that the coach must relate to the context in which the "other" is reasoning—they must "tune in" to where the other is coming from. In short, perhaps the basis of leadership is the capacity of the leader to change the mind-set, the framework of the other. That's not easy, as I needn't tell you for most of us, thinking that we have tuned into the other person, usually we are listening most intently to ourselves.

We were working with a financial services CEO named Lance who had difficulties with his four-woman major account team. They didn't care for him and didn't trust him and dreaded every meeting with him as he would go over their shortcomings.

Lance was at his wit's end and asked for coaching.

"Meet with each of them one at a time," we advised.

"What do I say?"

"Say nothing. Just listen."

"Listen to what?"

"The person across from you."

"What's my agenda?"

"No agenda."

"What do I ask them?"

"*How is life? How is life for you in this company? What would you change?*"

"Then what?"

"Then just listen."

"I don't know if I could do that."

The source of his major account team's low morale had just been identified. The rest was up to Lance.

4. Be the Cause, Not the Effect

> Shallow people believe in luck. Wise and strong
> people believe in cause and effect.
> —Ralph Waldo Emerson

A masterful motivator of others asks, "What do we want to *cause* to happen today? What do we want to produce?"

Those are the best management questions of all. People who have a hard time managing people simply have a hard time asking themselves those two questions, because they're always thinking about what's happening *to them* instead of what they're going to cause to happen.

When your people see you as a *cause* instead of an effect, it won't be hard to teach them to think the same way. Soon, you will be causing them to play far beyond their own self-concepts.

You can cause that to happen.

5. Stop Criticizing Upper Management

> Two things are bad for the heart—running uphill and
> running down people. —Bernard Gimbel

It is a huge temptation to distance yourself from your own superiors.

Maybe you do this to win favor and create bonding at the victim level with the team, but it won't work. In fact, what you have done will eventually damage the confidence of the team. It will send three messages that are very damaging to morale and motivation:

1. This organization can't be trusted.

2. Our own management is against us.

3. Yours truly, your own team leader, is weak and powerless in the organization.

This leads to a definite but unpleasant kind of bonding, and it leads to deep trust problems and further disrespect for the integrity of the organization. Running down upper management can be done covertly (a rolling of the eyes at the mention of the CFO's name) or overtly ("I don't know why we're doing this; no one ever consults with me on company policy, probably because they know I'd disagree"). This mistake is deepened by the repeated use of the word *they*. ("*They* want us to start...." "I don't know why *they* are having us do it this way...." "*They* don't understand what you guys are going through here...." "*They, they, they....*").

The word *they* used in excess soon becomes a near-obscenity and solidifies the impression that we are isolated, misunderstood victims.

A true leader has the courage to *represent* upper management, not run it down. **A true leader says *we*.**

6. Do the One Thing

> Management is doing things right; leadership is
> doing the right things. —Peter Drucker

I can't motivate others if I am not doing the right thing. And to keep myself in a relaxed and centered state, it's important for me to not be scattered, distracted, or spread thin. It's important that I don't race around thinking that I've got too much to do. I don't have too much to do. The truth is, *there is only one thing to do,* and that is the one thing I have chosen to do right now.

If I do that one thing as if it's all I have to think about, it will be extremely well done, and my relationship with any other person involved will be better and more relaxed and full of trust than before.

A careful study of my past week shows me that I did a lot of things, and they all got done one thing at a time. In fact, even in my busiest time ever, I was only able to do one thing at a time, even though I stressed myself and other people out by always thinking of seven things at once. When I talked to someone all I could think about was the seven other people I needed to talk to. Eventually, all seven people felt that stress and that lack of attentiveness, that absolute lack of warmth. Doing more than one thing at a time produces fear, adrenaline, and anxiety in the human system, and people pick up on that. People are not drawn to that. They keep away from that.

The mind entertains one thought at a time, and only one. The greatest cause of feeling "swamped" and "overwhelmed" in life is not knowing this.

The greatest source of stress in the workplace is the mind's attempt to carry many thoughts, many tasks, many future scenarios, many cares, many worries, many concerns at once. The mind can't do that. No mind can; not even Einstein's could.

I need to choose from the list of things that need to be done, and then do the one thing as if that were the only thing. If it's a phone call, then I need to slow down and relax and let myself be in a good mood so that the phone call will be a good experience, and the recipient and I can be complete afterward.

We talked to Jason, a national sales manager who had just finished a brutally long phone conference with his team. He spent the conference call nervously urging his team on to higher numbers and warning them that the team goals were not going to be met at the rate they were going. He had called the meeting because his own superiors had just called *him* to question him about his team's poor performance.

Although Jason had been working 12-hour days, he felt he was falling behind in everything. On top of that, his superiors' anxiety was then passed down to him. Because it was passed down into a hectic, disorganized mind, he freaked out and took it out on his team.

This is not motivation. Motivation requires a calm, centered leader who is focused on one thing, and only one thing.

Ps 107:30, Ps 131:2, Eccl 10:4

7. Keep Giving Feedback

> The failure to give appropriate and timely feedback is the most extreme cruelty that we can inflict on any human being. —Charles Coonradt, management consultant

Human beings crave feedback. Try ignoring any 3-year-old. At first, he will ask for positive attention, but if he is continually ignored, soon you will hear a loud crash or cry, because *any feedback, even negative feedback, is better than no feedback.*

Some people think that principle only applies to children. But it applies even more to adults. The cruelest form of punishment in prison is solitary confinement. Most prisoners will do *anything*—even temporarily improve their behavior—to avoid being in a situation with little or no feedback.

You may have briefly experienced the relaxing effect of a sensory deprivation chamber. You are placed for a few minutes in a dark, cocoon-like chamber, floating in body-temperature saltwater, with all light and sound cut off. It's great for a few minutes. But not for long.

One day the sole worker at one of these sensory-deprivation tanks walked off the job in a huff over some injustice at work, leaving a customer trapped in the chamber. Several hours later, the customer was rescued, but still had to be hospitalized. Not from any physical abuse, but from the psychosis caused by deprivation of sensory feedback. What occurs when all outside feedback is cut off is that the mind manufactures its own sensory feedback in the form of hallucinations that often personify the person's worst fears. The resulting nightmares and terrors can drive even normal people to the point of insanity.

Your own people are no different. If you cut off the feedback, their minds will manufacture their own feedback, quite often based on their worst fears. It's no accident that trust and communication are the two organizational problems most often cited by employee surveys.

Human beings crave *real* feedback, not just some patronizing, pacifying words. The managers who have the biggest trouble motivating their people are the ones who give the least feedback. And when their people ask, "How are we doing?" they say, "Well I don't know, I haven't looked at the printout or anything, but I have a *sense* that we're doing pretty well this month."

Those managers have a much harder time inspiring achievement in their teams. Achievement requires continuous feedback. And if you're going to get the most out of your people, it's imperative that you be the one who is the most up on what the numbers are and what they mean. Motivators do their homework. They know the score. And they keep feeding the score back to their people.

8. Get Input From Your People

> I not only use all the brains I have, but all I can borrow.—Woodrow Wilson

Good leaders continue to seek creative input from their direct reports. This practice is not only good for the business, it's also highly motivational for both parties to the conversation.

A good leader will ask people on her team, "How can we send a signal over the phone, when the customer calls with a question, that we are different than the other companies, and they are going to feel more welcome and at home with us? How do we create a relationship right there at the point of that call? What are your thoughts on this?"

The quality of our motivational skill is directly related to the quality of our questions.

A frustrated manager whose numbers are mediocre asks these kinds of questions instead of the questions just asked by our good leader:

"How ya doin'? What's up? How was your weekend? How is your department today? Up to your neck in it? Swamped as usual? Are you maintaining? Hang in there. Customers givin' you a hard time about that new ad? Jerks. I'm dropping by to check some stuff out. Don't worry too much, you guys are cool. I won't be too hard on you. You know the drill. Hang in."

That's a leader who can't figure out why his team's numbers are low. The quality of that leader's life is directly affected by the low quality of his questions. Directly. A great leader will ask questions that lead to sales ideas.

Questions such as: "How can we make the buying experience at our company fundamentally different, on a personal level, than at the competition? How can we get our people to be like friends to the customer and get them to hang out with us more and buy more? How might we reward our people for remembering a customer's name? What are some of the ways we can inspire our team to get excited about increasing the size of each sale? Do our people discuss the concept of creating a customer for life? Have you gone to a white board and shown them the financial windfall involved? How do we get everybody brainstorming this all day long? How do we get the team more involved in the success of the store? What are your thoughts?" A great leader will build a big success on the implementation of those ideas.

9. Accelerate Change

> Every organization must be prepared to abandon
> everything it does to survive in the future.
> —Peter Drucker

My role as a leader is *always* to keep my people cheered up, optimistic, and ready to play full-out in the face of change. That's my job. Most managers do not do this. They see their role as babysitters, problem-solvers, and firefighters. And so they produce babies, problems, and fires all around them.

It's important to know the psychological reaction to change in your employees and how it follows a predictable cycle.

Your employees pass through these four stages in the cycle, and you can learn how to manage this process:

The Change Cycle

1. Objection: "This can't be good."

2. Reduced consciousness: "I really don't want to deal with this."

3. Exploration: "How can I make this change work for me?"

4. Buy-in: "I have figured out how I can make this work for me and for others."

Sometimes the first three stages in the cycle take a long time for your people to pass through. Productivity and morale can take a dizzying dip as employees resist change. It is human nature to resist change. We all do it.

If I am a very good leader, I want to thoroughly understand the change cycle so that I can get my people to "buy-in" as soon as humanly possible. I want their total and deep buy-in to make this change work for them, for me, and for the company.

So how do I help move them through stages one, two, and three? First of all, I prepare myself to communicate about this change in the most enthusiastic and positive way possible. And I mean prepare. As many great coaches have said, "It isn't the will to win that wins the game, it's *the will to prepare* to win." I want to arm myself. I want to educate and inform myself about the change so I can be an enthused spokesperson in favor of the change.

Most managers don't do this. They realize that their people are resisting the change, so they identify with the loyal resistance. They sympathize with the outcry. They give voice to what a hassle the change is. They even apologize for it. They say it shouldn't have happened.

"This never should have happened. I'm sorry. With all you people go through. What a shame there's this now, too."

Every internal change is made to improve the viability or effectiveness of the company. Those arguments are the ones I want to sell. I want my people to see what's in this for *them*. I want them to really see for themselves that a more viable company is a more secure place to work.

What about change from the outside? Regulators, market shifts, vendor problems? In those cases, I want to stress to my team that the competition faces the same changes. When it rains on the field, it rains on both teams. Then I want to stress the superiority of our team's rain strategy, so that this rain becomes our advantage.

I also want to keep change alive on my team as a positive habit. Yes, we change all the time. We change before we have to.

10. Know Your Owners and Victims

Those who follow the part of themselves that is great will become great. Those that follow the part that is small will become small. —Mencius

The people you motivate will tend to divide themselves into two categories: owners and victims.

This distinction comes from Steve's *Reinventing Yourself,* which revealed in detail how *owners* are people who take full responsibility for their happiness, and *victims* are always lost in their unfortunate stories. Victims blame others, blame circumstance, and are hard to deal with. Owners own their own morale. They own their response to any situation.

At a seminar, a company CEO named Marcus approached Steve at the break:

"I have a lot of victims working for me," Marcus said.

"It's a part of our culture," Steve answered.

"Yeah, I know, but how can I get them to recognize their victim tendencies?"

"Try something else instead," Steve said. "Try getting excited when they are *not* victims. Try pointing out their ownership actions; try acknowledging them when they are pro-active and self-responsible."

"Okay. What are the best techniques to use with each type of person?" Marcus asked. "I mean, I have both. I have owners, too. Do you treat them differently?"

"With the owners in your life, you don't need techniques. Just appreciate them," Steve said. "And you will. With the victims, be patient. Hear their feelings out empathetically. You can empathize with their feelings without buying in to their victim viewpoint. Show them the other view. Live it for them. They will see with their own eyes that it gets better results."

"Can't I just have you come in to give them a seminar in ownership?" Marcus said.

"In the end, even if we were to train your staff in owner-ship thinking, you would still have to lead them there every day, or it would be easy to lose. Figure out your own ways to lead them there. Design ways that incorporate your own personality and style into it. There is no magic prescription. There is only commitment. People who are committed to having a team of self-responsible, creative, upbeat people will get exactly that. Leaders whose commitment isn't there won't get it. The three basic things you can do are: 1) reward ownership wherever you see it. 2) be an owner yourself. 3) take full responsibility for your staff's morale and performance."

Marcus looked concerned. We could tell he still wasn't buying everything.

"What's troubling you?" Steve asked.

"Don't be offended."

"Of course not."

"How do I turn around a victim without appearing to be that annoying 'positive thinker'?"

"You don't have to come off as an annoying positive thinker to be a true leader. Just be realistic, honest, and upbeat. Focus on opportunities and possibilities. Focus on the true and realistic upside. Don't gossip or run down other people. There is no reliable trick that always works, but in our experience, when you are a really strong example of ownership, and you clearly acknowledge it, reward it, and notice it in other people (especially in meetings, where victims can hear you doing it), it gets harder and harder for people to play victim in that setting. Remember that being a victim is essentially a racket. It is a manipulation. You don't have to pretend that it's a valid point of view intellectually, because it is not."

"Okay, I see. That sounds doable," Marcus said. "But there's one new employee I'm thinking about. He started out great for a few months, but now he seems so lost and feels betrayed. That's his demeanor, anyway. How do I instill a sense of ownership in him?"

[handwritten, left margin, top: "are not willing to do. ~Me"]

[handwritten, left margin vertical: "Never ask anyone to do whatever you yourself"]

"You really can't 'instill' it. Not directly. Ownership, by its nature, is grown by the owner. But you can encourage it, and nourish it when you see it. You can nurture it and reward it. You can even celebrate it. If you do all those things, it will appear, like a flower in your garden. You don't make it grow, but if you do certain things, it will appear." *[handwritten: 1 Cor 3: 6-9]*

11. Lead From the Front

> You can't change people. You must be the change you wish to see in people. —Gandhi

There is nothing more motivational than leading from the front.

✷ It motivates others when you are out there and you do it yourself. It's inspiring to them when you do what you want them to do. Be inspiring. Your people would rather be inspired than fixed or corrected. They would rather be inspired than anything else.

[handwritten: Ha! See next page! Gen Patton!]

As a motivational practice, leading from the front hits harder and lasts longer than any other practice. It changes people more deeply and more completely than anything else you can do.

So *be* what you want to see.

If you want your people to be more positive, be more positive. If you want them to take more pride in their work, take more pride in yours. Show them how it's done. Want them to look good and dress professionally? Look better yourself. Want them to be on time? Always be early (and tell them why—tell them what punctuality means to *you*).

And as General George Patton used to say, "There are three principles of leadership: 1) example, 2) example, and 3) example."

12. Preach the Role of Thought

Great men are they who see that thought is stronger than any material force, that thoughts rule the world.

—Ralph Waldo Emerson

Phil 4:7

Business and life coach and psychic intuitive JacQuaeline told us this story last week about a mechanic in a school district complaining of having punched the clock and doing the same thing on his job over and over for the last 20 years.

"I'm burned out and need a change!" the mechanic declared.

"Possibly," JacQuaeline replied. "But you might want to try learning to love what you are resisting, because if you don't, you will likely run into it in your next job, too, in another guise."

The mechanic responded, "I'm not sure that I believe that, but even if I did, how is that possible?"

"Well," his coach said, "what is a higher purpose to your job than just turning nuts and bolts every day?"

"That's easy," replied the mechanic. "The higher purpose of my job is saving children's lives every day."

"Yes, that's great!" whispered the coach. "Now, every morning when you get into your higher purpose, saving children's lives every day, you will be clear that your job and responsibility is so important that the time clock almost won't matter anymore."

She had given him a new way to think. She had put him in touch with the power of thought to transform experience.

Make certain all the people you want to motivate understand the role of *thought* in life. There is nothing more important.

Why is it that the rain depresses one person and makes another person happy?

If things "make you" feel something, why does this thing called rain make one person feel one thing and the other person feel the other thing? Why, if things make you feel something, doesn't the rain make both people feel the same thing? One person you lead might say, "Oh no, bad weather, how depressing." Another person might say, "Oh boy, we have some wonderful, refreshing rain!"

The rain doesn't make either person feel anything. (No person, place, or thing can make you feel anything.) It is *the thought about the rain* that causes the feelings. And throughout all your leadership adventures, you can teach your people this most important concept: the concept of thought.

One person thinks the rain is great. The other person thinks the rain is depressing. Nothing in the world has any meaning until we give it meaning. Nothing in the workplace does, either. Your people often look to *you* for meaning. What does this new directive really mean?

Do you sense the opportunity you have?

We can make things mean anything we want them to, within reason. Why not use that power?

People don't make your employees angry; their own thoughts make them angry. They can't be angry unless they think the thoughts that make them angry.

If your employer wins the lottery in the morning, who's going to make her angry that day? No one. No matter what anyone says to her, she isn't going to care. She's not going to give it another thought. Your employees can only get angry with someone if they *think* about that person and what he is saying and doing and what a threat it is to their happiness. If they don't think about that, how can they be angry?

Your people are free to think about anything they want. They have absolute freedom of thought.

The highest IQ ever measured in any human being was achieved by Marilyn vos Savant, many years in a row. Once someone asked Marilyn what the relationship was between feeling and thinking. She said, "Feeling is what you get for thinking the way you do."

Marcus Aurelius wrote in AD 150, "The soul becomes dyed with the color of its thoughts."

People feel motivated only when they think motivated thoughts. Thought rules. Circumstance does not rule. The closer your relationship to that truth, the better the leader you are.

13. Tell the Truth Quickly

Question: How many legs does a dog have if you call the tail a leg? Answer: Four; calling a tail a leg doesn't make it a leg. —Abraham Lincoln

Great leaders always share a common habit: They tell the truth more quickly than other managers do.

Steve recalls his work with helping managers motivate salespeople. But it doesn't just apply to salespeople. It applies to all people.

I always found that people would tell me about their limitations, and I would patiently listen and try to talk them out of their limitations, and they would try to talk me back into what their limitations really were. That seemed to be their obsession.

One day, I was working with a salesperson in a difficult one-on-one coaching session, and finally I just blurted it out (I guess I was tired, or upset, or was having a stressful day) and I said, "You know, you're just lying to me."

"What?" he said.

"You're lying. Don't tell me there's nothing you can do. There's *a lot* you can do. So let's you and I work with the truth, because if we work with the truth and we don't lie to each other, we are going to get to your success more quickly than if we do it this way, focusing on your self-deceptions."

Well, my client was absolutely shocked. He stared at me for a long time. It's not always a great relationship-builder to call someone a liar. I don't recommend it. If I hadn't been as tired as I was, I don't think I would have done it, but the remarkable thing was, my client all of a sudden began to smile! He sat back in his chair and he said, "You know what? You are right."

I said, "What?"

He said, "I said, you know what, you are right, that's not the truth at all, is it?"

"No, it's not."

"You are right," he said, "There's a lot I can do."

"Yes, there is."

Jn 8:44, 45

This is the main lie you hear in the world of business and especially in sales: "There's nothing I can do." This is the "I am helpless and powerless" lie. The truth is, there is always a lot you can do. You just have to choose the most creative and efficient way to do it. As Shakespeare wrote, "Action is eloquence."

One way a salesperson I know starts her day off with action is to ask herself, "If I were coaching me, what would I advise myself to do right now? What creative, service-oriented, beneficial action could I take that my client would be grateful for in the end? What action would bring the highest return to me?"

Another quick cure for the feeling that "there's nothing I can do" is to ask yourself, "If I were my customer or my prospect, what would I want me to do?"

Great salespeople, and any people who lead their teams in performance and who prosper the most from their profession, are great givers. They stay in constant touch with their power to *do so much* by constantly giving their internal and external clients beneficial things—helpful information, offers of service, respect for their time, support for their success, cheerful and friendly encounters, sincere acknowledgments, the inside scoop—giving, giving, giving all day long, always putting the client's wants and needs first. They always ask the best questions and always listen better than anyone else listens. As that commitment grows and expands, and those gifts are lavished on each client in creative and ongoing communications, that salesperson becomes a world-class expert in client psychology and buying behavior. And that salesperson also realizes that such a dizzying level of expertise can only be acquired through massive benefit-based interaction!

A new week begins, and this thought occurs: "There's *so* much good I can do, I just can't wait."

14. Don't Confuse Stressing With Caring

> Stress, in addition to being itself and the result of
> itself, is also the cause of itself.
> —Hans Selye, psychologist

Titus 3:8

Most managers try double negatives as a way to motivate others. First they intentionally upset themselves over the prospect of *not* reaching their goals, and then they use the upset as negative energy to fire up the team.

It doesn't work.

Stressing out over our team's goals is not the same as caring about them. Stressing out is not a useful form of motivation. No performer, when tense or stressed, performs well. No leader does. No salesperson. No athlete. No fund-raiser. No field-goal kicker. No free-throw shooter. No parent.

A stressed-out, tense performer only has access to a small percent of his or her skill and intelligence. If your favorite team is playing, do you want a tense, stressed-out person shooting a free throw or kicking a long field goal in the last moments of the game? Or would you rather see a confident, calm player step up to the challenge?

Most people stress themselves out as a form (or a show) of "really caring" about hitting some goal. But it's not caring, it's stressing out. Stressing out makes one do worse. True caring makes one do better. That's why it's vital for a leader to know the difference. The two couldn't be more different.

Caring is relaxing, focusing, and calling on *all* of your resources, all of that relaxed magic, that lazy dynamite that you bring to bear when you pay full attention with peace of mind. No one performs better than when he or she is relaxed and focused.

[handwritten margin notes: "it feeds on itself", "I worked pmc to power up", "down", "V.S. wanted to know why the thought I asked it", "The more stressed I get the quieter I get"]

"Stress is basically a disconnection from the Earth," says the great creativity teacher Natalie Goldberg. "It's a forgetting of the breath. Stress is an ignorant state. It believes that everything is an emergency. Nothing is that important. Just lie down."

It is not necessary to stress, only to focus and remain focused. Anything you pay attention to will expand. Just don't spend your attention any old place. Spend it where you want the greatest results: on clients, customers, money, whatever. In a relaxed and happy way, be relentless, undivided, peaceful, and powerful. You will succeed.

15. Manage Your Own Superiors

> There is no such thing as constructive criticism.
> —Dale Carnegie

Jean was an administrator in a large hospital system we were working with. She welcomed the coaching work we were doing, but had a pressing question about her own leadership.

"We have had a lot of different bosses to report to," Jean said. "It seems that just when we're used to working for a certain CEO, the hospital brings in someone new."

"What exactly is the problem with that?" we asked.

"Well, with so many changes in leadership over the years," Jean asked, "how do we develop trust in the process?"

"By trusting the process. Trust is not the same as verification. Trust risks something. And it is not necessarily bad or good that leadership changes. The question is, can you teach yourself to live and work with the change? It's not whether it has changed so much but rather this: What are you going to do to capitalize on the change?"

"What if we don't like the leadership now?" she pressed on.

"What don't you like?"

"We get mixed messages from them!" Jean said. "And how can you keep asking us to take ownership when we get mixed messages from senior management?"

"Every large organization we have ever worked with has had to confront, in varying degrees, this issue of 'mixed messages.' Mixed messages happen because people are only human and it's hard to coordinate a lot of energetic creative people to present themselves as one."

"I agree," said Jean. "But it's a challenge."

"It's a challenge that must be dealt with. But it is not necessary to use it as a source of defeat or depression. It's a challenge. We have often seen the 'message from the top' become more coherent and unified when the request for unity 'from below' becomes more benevolent and creative."

"You're saying I should manage *them* a little better," Jean said.

"Exactly."

"With the key words being 'benevolent' and 'creative'?"

"Those would be the key words."

16. Put Your Hose Away

Wise leaders and high achievers come to understand that they can't hope to eliminate problems...and wouldn't want to. —Dale Dauten

Why are so many managers ineffective leaders?

Because they are firefighters. When you become a firefighter, you don't lead anymore. You don't decide where your team is going. The fire decides for you. (The *fire* is whatever current problem has flared up and captured your time and imagination.)

The fire controls your life. You think you are controlling the fire, but the fire is controlling you. You become unconscious of opportunity. You become blind to possibilities, because you are immersed in, and defined, by the fire.

If you're an unmotivational manager, even when you put the fire out, you hop back on the truck and take off across the company looking for another fire. Soon, *all you know is fires,* and all you know how to do is fight them. Even when there is no real fire, you'll find something to *redefine* as a fire because you are a firefighter and always want to be working.

A great motivator doesn't fight fires 24/7. A true motivator leads people from the present into the future. The only time a fire becomes relevant is when it's in the way of that future goal. Sometimes a leader doesn't even have to put the fire out. Sometimes she just takes a path around (or above) the fire to get to the desired future.

A firefighter, on the other hand, will stop everything and fight every fire. That's the basic difference between an unconscious manager (letting the fires dictate activity) and a conscious leader (letting desired goals dictate activity).

17. Get the Picture

People cannot be managed... Inventories can be managed, but people must be led. —H. Ross Perot

Here's a common question: Isn't leadership something people are born with? Aren't some people referred to as *born leaders*?

Yes, but it's a myth. Leadership is a skill, like gardening or chess or playing a computer game. It can be taught and it can be learned at any age if the commitment to learn is present. Companies *can* turn their managers into leaders.

But if companies could transform all their managers into leaders, why wouldn't every company just do that?

They don't know what a leader is, most of them. They don't read books on leadership, they don't have leadership training seminars, and they don't hold meetings in which leadership is discussed and brainstormed. Therefore, they can't define it. It's hard to encourage it or cultivate it if you can't define it.

The remedy for this is to always have a picture of what a good leader is. People are not motivated by people who can't picture great leadership. Can't even picture it!

In his powerful, innovative book on business management, *The Laughing Warriors* (Lumina Media, 2003), Dale Dauten offers a picture of a leader with a code to live by: "THINK LIKE A HERO (who can I help today?), WORK LIKE AN ARTIST (what else can we try?), REFUSE TO BE ORDINARY (pursue excellence, then kill it.), and CELEBRATE (but take no credit.)."

Continuously picturing that code in and of itself would create quite a leader.

18. Manage Agreements, Not People

Those that are most slow in making a promise are the
most faithful in the performance of it.
—Jean-Jacques Rousseau

"Does anybody here work with people who seem unmanageable?" Steve Chandler asked as he opened one of his leadership seminars.

The managers who filled the room nodded and smiled in
agreement. Some rolled their eyes skyward in agreement. They
obviously had a lot of experience trying to manage people like
that.

"How do you do it?" one manager called out. "How do you
manage unmanageable people?"

"I don't know," Steve said.

"What do you mean you don't know? We're here to find out
how to do it," someone else called out.

"I've never seen it done," Steve said. "Because I believe, in
the end, all people are pretty unmanageable. I've never known
anyone who was good at managing people."

"Then why have a seminar on managing people if it can't
be done?"

"Well, you tell me: can it be done? Do you actually manage your people? Do you manage your spouse? Can you do it?
I don't think so."

"Well, then, is class dismissed?"

"No, certainly not. Because we can all stay and learn how
great leaders get great results from their people. But they do it

without managing people, because basically you can't manage people."

"If they don't manage people, what do they do?"

"They manage agreements."

Managers make a mistake when they try to manage their people. They end up trying to shovel mercury with a pitchfork, managing people's emotions and personalities. Then they try to "take care" of their most upset people, not in the name of better communication and understanding, but in the name of containing dissent and being liked. This leads to poor time management and a lot of ineffective amateur psychotherapy. It also encourages employees to take a more immature position in their communication with management, almost an attempt to be re-parented by a supervisor rather than having an adult relationship.

A leader's first responsibility is to make sure the relationship is a mature one.

A true leader does not run around playing amateur psychotherapist, trying to manage people's emotions and personalities all day. A leader is compassionate, and always seeks to understand the feelings of others. But a leader does not try to *manage* those feelings. Instead, a leader manages agreements. A leader creates agreements with team members and enters into those agreements on an adult-to-adult basis. All communication is done with respect. There is no giving in to the temptation to be intimidating, bossy, or all-knowing.

Once agreements are made on an adult-to-adult basis, people don't have to be managed anymore. What gets managed are the agreements. It is more mature and respectful to do it that way, and both sides enjoy more open and trusting communication. There is also more accountability running both ways. It is now easier to discuss uncomfortable subjects.

Harry was an employee who always showed up late for team meetings. Many managers would deal with this problem by talking behind Harry's back, or trying to intimidate Harry with sarcasm, or freezing Harry out and not return his calls, or meeting with Harry to play therapist. But our client Jill would do none of that.

Jill cogenerated an agreement with Harry that Harry (and Jill) would be on time for meetings. They agreed to agree, and they agreed to keep their commitments to the agreements. It is an adult process that leads to open communication and relaxed accountability. Jill has come to realize that when adults agree to keep their agreements with each other, it leads to a more openly accountable company culture. It leads to higher levels of self-responsibility and self-respect.

The biggest beneficial impact of managing agreements is on communication. It frees communication up to be more honest, open, and complete. A commitment to managing agreements is basically a commitment to being two professional adults working together, as opposed to "I'm your dad/I'm your father/I'm your mother/I'm your parent/I will re-parent you/You're a child/You're bad/You've done wrong/I'm upset with you/I'm disappointed in you, and I know that you've got your reasons, but still, I'm disappointed in you." That kind of approach is not management, it's not leadership. It's not even professional. That kind of approach, which we would say eight out of 10 managers do, is just a knee jerk, intuitively parent-child approach to managing human beings.

The problem with parent-child management is that the person being managed does not feel respected in that exchange.

And the most important, the most powerful precondition to good performance is trust and respect.

Let's say my team has agreed to do something. They've all agreed to watch a video and then take a certain test given on the Internet. But then they don't do it! What does it mean that they won't do things like that? What does it say about them? What does it say about me?

All it means is that the person in charge of getting that project done is someone with whom I need to strengthen my agreement. It's not someone who's done something "wrong." It's someone with whom I don't have a very strong agreement.

And so I need to sit down with each of them or get into a good phone conversation with each of them, and say, "You and I need an agreement on this because this is something that must be done, and I want to have it done in the way that you can do it the most effectively, that won't get in the way of your day-to-day work. So let's talk about this. Let me help you with this so that it does get done. It's not an option, so you and I must come up with a way together that we can both coauthor, together, an agreement on how this is going to get done."

Then I should ask the following questions of that person: "Are you willing to do this? Is this something you can make people follow up on? Can you make sure people do this? Do you have a way of doing it? Do you need my support?"

And finally, at the end of the conversation, I've got that person agreeing with me about the project.

Now, notice that this agreement is two-sided. So I also, as the coprofessional in this agreement, am agreeing to certain things, too.

That person might have said, "You know, one of the hard things about this is we don't have anything to watch this video on; we don't have a TV monitor in the store."

And so I would say, "If I can get you a TV for your store, will that be all you need?"

"Yes, it will."

"Well, here's what you can count on. By Friday, I'll have a TV monitor in the store. What else can I do for you?"

A leader is always serving, too. Not just laying down the law, but serving. A leader is always asking, "How can I assist you? How can I serve you and help you with this?" The true leader wants an absolute promise, and absolute performance. And now that the two people have agreed, I ask very sincerely, "Can I count on you now to have this done, with 100-percent compliance? Can I count on that from you?"

"Yes, of course you can."

Great. We shake. Two professionals leaving a meeting with an agreement they both made out of mutual respect, out of professional, grown-up conversation. Nobody was managed.

19. Focus on the Result, Not the Excuse

A leader has to be able to change an organization that is dreamless, soulless and visionless...someone's got to make a wake up call. —Warren Bennis

If you are a sales manager, you probably run into the same frustrations that Frank did when he talked to us from San Francisco.

"I believe I need advice on how to deliver the 'Just Do It' message to my people," Frank said. "I've said it every way I can, and I think I'm starting to sound like a broken record. I don't know why I called you. I thought maybe you were advising your clients to pick up some new book to read, or that you might have some general words of wisdom."

"What, specifically, is your problem?"

"Half of the people on the team I manage are total non-producers!" he said. "And I keep telling them...it's not magical... it's getting the leads...and getting it done...."

"I've said, 'Just get off your butt, go get referrals, make 60 to 75 phone calls, visit with eight to 10 potential buyers each week, and watch how successful you'll be.'"

"What's really missing here?" we asked him. "What's wrong with your picture? Why aren't they out there doing what would lead to sales?"

"That's why I called you. If I *knew what was missing*, I wouldn't have called you."

"Because it isn't 'just doing it' that is missing from the non-producers' equation. Although we always think it is. What's really missing runs deeper than that. What's really missing is the 'just *wanting* it.'"

"Oh, I know they all say they want it. They want the commissions and they want the success."

"They don't want it, or they would have it."

"Oh, so you think people get everything they want?"

"Actually, yes, they do."

"Really? I don't see that."

"That's what we humans are all about. We know how to get what we want. We are biological systems designed to do that."

We talked longer. There was something we wanted Frank to see: Frank's non-producers were underproducing because they did not *want* to produce. If you are a manager you must understand that. If you are a non-producer, you must understand that.

Non-producers are not in sales to focus all their attention on succeeding at selling. If they were, they would be producers. Even if they say they are focused on results, they're not. They are in sales because of other reasons...they believe they need the money, maybe, and therefore think they *should* be there.

But they can't get any intellectual or motivational leverage from *should*. *Should* sets them up for failure. It implies that they are still children, and that they are trying to live up to other people's expectations. There's no power in that. No focus. No leverage.

Salespeople who do what they think they *should* do all day convert their managers into their parents. Then they age-regress into childhood and whine and complain. Even when you try to micromanage their activities, even when you are eloquent in showing them that Activity A leads to Result B (always) and Result B leads to Result C (always), they still do it half-heartedly and search in vain for a new "how to" from other mentors and producers.

Frank began to see this form of dysfunction quite clearly, but he still didn't know what to do about it. Frank needed to manage the *want to*, not the *how to*. Frank needed a quick course in outcome-management because, like most people, he was stuck in the world of process-management. The real joy of leadership can only come when you're getting results.

"Tell me what I as a manager ought to do," he said, after he realized that he already understood this whole idea.

"Once you get the non-producer's sales goal (plan, quota, numbers) in front of you for mutual discussion," we said, "you need to draw out and cultivate the *why*. Why do you want this? What will it do for you? What else will it do for you? What's one thing more it will do for you? If we were to tell you that there were activities that would absolutely get you to this number, would you do these activities? If not, why not? Would you promise me and yourself that you would do these activities until you hit the number? Why or why not?"

If you're a manager like Frank, please keep in mind that you have people who don't really want what they are telling you they want, and even they don't realize that. You know that if they truly wanted to be producers, nothing in the world could stop them.

Intention Deficit Disorder is what we have named the dysfunction that is always at the core of non-production. It is not a deficit in technique or know-how. Technique and know-how are *hungrily* acquired by the person who has an absolute and focused intention to succeed.

The real long-term trick to good management is to hire people who want success. Once you have mastered that tricky art form, you will always succeed. But we get lazy in the hiring process and look for and listen for all the wrong things.

Why do we do this? Why do we miss this crucial lack of desire in the hiring process? This is why: people we hire really have a big "want to" when it comes to getting the job. They really want the job. However, this is distinctly different than wanting to succeed at the job. These are two completely different goals. So we are lazy in the interviewing process, only half-listening to them, and we mistake their burning desire to *get the job* with a burning desire to succeed. It is a completely different thing.

The best managers we have ever trained always took more time and trouble in the hiring process than any of their competitors did. Then, once they had hired ambitious people, they based their management on the management of those people's *personal* goals. When sales managers learned to link the activity of cold-calling to the salesperson's most specific personal goals, for example, cold-calling became something much more meaningful. These managers were spending their days managing results, not activities. Their positive reinforcement was always for results, not for activities.

20. Coach the Outcome

Unless commitment is made, there are only promises
and hopes...but no plans. —Peter Drucker

Every non-producer you are managing is in some form of conflict. They want to succeed and hit their numbers, but their activity says otherwise. They themselves can't even see it, but you, the manager, can, and it drives you nuts. You have that talk that you always have, during which you say to them, "I have a feeling that I want this for you more than you want it for yourself." They get misty-eyed and their tears well up while they insist you are wrong. And you, being such a compassionate person, believe them! So you give them yet another chance to prove it to you. You do all kinds of heroics for them and waste all your time on them when your time could be better spent with your producers.

Always remember that the time you spend helping a producer helps your team's production *more* than the time you spend with your non-producer.

Some research we have seen shows that managers spend more than 70 percent of their time trying to get non-producers to produce. And most producers, when they quit for another job, quit because they didn't get enough attention. They didn't feel that they were appreciated enough by the company, nor could they grow fast enough in their position.

If you help a producer who is selling 10 muffins a week learn how to sell 15, you have moved him up to 150 percent of his former level, and, even better, you have added five muffins to your team's total. If you were to spend that time, instead, with a non-producer, and get her up to 150 percent, you might have just moved her up from two muffins to three. You've only added one muffin (instead of five) to the team total. Most managers spend most of their days with the non-producer...adding *one muffin* to the team's total.

Managers need to simplify, simplify, simplify. They do not need to do what they normally do: complicate, multitask, and complicate.

Keep it as simple as you can for your non-producers, focusing on outcomes and results only. Spend more and more time with producers who are looking for that extra edge you can give them.

Non-producers have a huge lesson to learn from you. They could be learning every day that their production is a direct result of their own desire (or lack of it) to hit that precise number. People figure out ways to get what they want. Most non-producers want to keep their jobs (because of their spouse's disapproval if they lose it, because of their fear of personal shame if they lose it, and so on), so all their activity is directed at *keeping the job* from one month to the next. If they can do the minimum in sales and still keep their job, they are getting what they want. People get what they want.

The manager's challenge is to redirect all daily effort toward hitting a precise number. If your people believed that they *had* to hit that number, they would hit that number, and technique would never be an issue. Skills would never be an issue. They would find them. They would try out every technique in the book until that number appeared. Somehow, non-producers have convinced themselves that there is no direct cause and effect between increasing certain activities and hitting their number.

Do you remember those little toy robots or cars you had when you were a kid that would bump into a wall and then turn 30 degrees and go again? And every time they bumped into something they would turn 30 degrees and go again. If you put one of those toys in a room with an open door, it will always find the way out the door. Always. It is programmed to do so. It is mechanically programmed to keep trying things until it is *out of there.* That's what top producers program themselves to do. It's the same thing. They keep trying stuff until they find a way. If they bump into a wall, they immediately turn 30 degrees and set out again.

The non-producer bumps into the wall and gets depressed and then shuts himself down. Sometimes for 20 minutes, sometimes for a whole day or week. Alternately, he bumps into a wall and doesn't turn in any other direction, so he keeps bumping into the same wall until his batteries run down.

Managers also make the mistake of buying in to their non-producers' perceived problems. They buy in to the non-producers' never-ending crusade to convince everyone that there is no cause and effect in their work. It's all a matter of luck! In fact, non-producers almost delight in bringing back evidence that there is no cause and effect. They tell you long case histories of all the activities they did that led to *nothing*. All the heartbreak. All the times they were *misled* by prospective buyers.

A manager's real opportunity is to teach his people absolute respect for personal responsibility for results. Everyone selling in the free market is 100-percent accountable for his or her financial situation. Every salesperson is *outcome*-accountable as well as activity-accountable.

Your non-producers will always want to sell you on what they have done, all the actions they have taken. What they don't want is to take responsibility for outcomes. Good sales management is outcome management, not activities management. Yet most sales managers go crazy all day managing activities.

Why? Because they *know* that if you really do these activities without ceasing, you *will* get results. So they manage the activities. They need to change that and manage results. They need to hold people accountable for the results they are getting, *not* how hard they are trying. The minute a manager falls for how hard people are trying, he has broken the cause and effect link.

If you as manager ask them, "How much X do you do?" they will ask, "How do I learn a better technique for X?" Although better techniques are always good, that's not the point here. You are now discussing results. They will subconsciously try to steer you away from results into technique. Just as a child does with a parent! "Dad I tried but I can't! I can't do it!" Discuss technique later, after the commitment to results is clarified.

Non-producers, at the deepest level, do not *want* to get the result. You have to understand this so you won't go crazy trying to figure them out. They don't want the result. They want the job. They want your approval. They want to be seen as "really trying." But deep down, they don't want the result. It's that simple.

Truly great managers spend most of their time helping good producers go from 10 muffins to 15. They have fun. They are creative. They feed off of their producers' skills and enthusiasm. Their teams constantly out-perform other teams. Why? Because other teams' managers have been hypnotized by their non-producers. Their non-producers actually become good salespeople selling the wrong thing. Selling you the *worst* thing: "There is *no* cause and effect...there is *no* guarantee."

Simplify. Focus on results. You will always get what you focus on. If you merely focus on activities, that's what you'll get...a whole lot of activities. But if you focus on results, that's what you'll get. A whole lot of results.

21. Create a Game

> Although some people think that life is a battle, it is
> actually a game of giving and receiving.
> —Florence Scovill Shinn, philosopher and author

Complete this sentence with the first word that pops into your head: "Life is a _____." Whatever comes to mind first, here's something that you (and we) can be sure of: That is exactly how life now seems to you.

What was your answer? In a poll of mid-level managers, the most common answer was: "Life is a battle." But in a poll of senior executives, the most common answer was: "Life is a game." Which version of life would you choose, if you had a choice?

To be as motivational a leader as you can possibly be, you might want to show your people that life with you is a game. What makes any activity a game? There needs to be some way to keep score, to tell whether people are winning or losing, and the result must not matter at all. Then it becomes pure fun. So be clear that although all kinds of prizes may be attached to the game, the game itself is being played for the sheer fun of it.

Chuck Coonradt, a long-time friend and mentor, is a management consultant and the best-selling author of *The Game of Work*. He has created an entire system for making a game out of work. Chuck recalled that when he started in the grocery business, in the icy frozen food section of the warehouse, he noticed that the owners would bend over backward to take care of their workers. They would give them breaks every hour to warm up and they would give them preferential pay. But no matter what they did, the workers would bitterly complain about the chilling cold.

"However, you could take these exact same workers and put a deer rifle into their hands," Chuck said, "and you could send them out into weather that was much worse than anything in the warehouse, and they would call it fun! And you wouldn't have to pay them a dime! In fact, they will pay for it themselves!"

Randy was a leader-client of ours who had a problem with absenteeism. For many months, he tried to attack and eliminate the problem. Finally, he realized that it is always possible to lighten things up by introducing the game element.

So Randy created a game. (Leaders create, managers react.) He issued a playing card to every employee with perfect attendance for the month. A card was drawn at random from a bucket of cards. The employee then hung the card up in his or her cubicle. At the end of six months, the person with the best poker hand won a major prize. The second, and third, best hands also won good cash prizes.

"My absenteeism problem virtually disappeared," Randy later recalled. "In fact, we had some problems with actual sick people trying to work when they shouldn't have. They would wake up with a fever, and their spouse would say, 'You're staying home today,' and they would say, 'Are you crazy? I'm holding two aces and two queens, and you want me to stay home?'"

After being in business for four years selling a pre-packaged management development program, Chuck Coonradt made what became the most important sales call of his career.

He called on a plant manager in a pre-constructed housing company. As part of their discussion, the manager began to give Chuck the "Kids Today" lecture—kids don't care, kids won't work, kids don't have the same values you and I had when we were growing up.

"As he was speaking, we were looking over the factory floor from the management office 30 feet above the factory floor," Chuck recalled. "He pointed down to the eight young men siding a house and said, 'What are you and your program going to do about that?'"

Chuck said that he looked at their work pace and said that it "would best be compared to arthritic snails in wet cement. These guys appeared to be two degrees out of reverse and leaning backwards! He had given me objections for which I didn't have an answer. I really didn't know what to say."

Then an amazing event occurred—lunch. As soon as the lunch bell rang, these eight workers dropped their hammers as if they were electrified, took off on a dead run as if being stuck with cattle prods, four of them taking off their shirts, running 50 yards down the factory floor to a basketball court.

The motivational transformation was amazing! Chuck watched the game, mesmerized, for exactly 42 minutes. Everybody knew their job on the court, did their job on the court, and supported the team with energy, engagement, and enthusiasm—all without management. They knew how to contribute to the team they were on, and they enjoyed it.

At 12:42 the game stopped, they picked up their sack lunches and their sodas and began to walk back to their work stations, where, at 1 p.m., they were back on the clock—arthritic snails back in the wet cement.

Chuck turned to the plant manager and said, "I don't believe there is a raw human material problem. I don't think there is anything wrong with these kids' motivation."

And on that day Chuck began a quest to see if it would be possible to transfer the energy, enthusiasm, and engagement that he saw on the basketball court to the factory work floor. His success at doing so has become legendary throughout the business world.

"Now we identify the *motivation of recreation* and bring it to the workplace," Chuck says. "The motivation of recreation includes feedback, scorekeeping, goal-setting, consistent coaching, and personal choice."

22. Know Your Purpose

> There is nothing so useless as doing efficiently that
> which should not be done at all. —Peter Drucker

It is hard to motivate others if you don't have time to talk to them. There are fewer discouraging sights than a leader who has become a true chicken running around with his head cut off—and not enough time to find it.

Managers whose teams are not performing up to expectations are simply doing ineffective things all day. Rather than stopping and deciding what would be the right thing to do, they do the wrong things faster and faster, stressing out more and more over the "workload." (There is no "workload" to worry about if you are doing the right thing. There is only that thing.)

And as corporate time-management specialist David Allen says of busy leaders: "You have more to do than you can possibly do. You just need to feel good about your choices."

Multitasking is the greatest myth in modern-day business. The thinking part of the brain itself does not multitask, and so people do not really multitask. The human system is not set up that way. The system has one thought at a time.

Managers often *think* they are multitasking, but they are really just doing one thing badly and then quickly moving to another thing, doing *it* badly and quickly. Soon they're preoccupied with all the tasks they've touched but left incomplete.

And, as business efficiency expert Kerry Gleeson has noted, "The constant, unproductive preoccupation with all the things we have to do is the single largest consumer of time and energy." Not the things we do, the things we leave undone.

People who find the joy in leadership find ways to relax into an extremely purposeful day, goal-oriented and focused on the highest-priority activity. They can think at any given moment: Sure they get distracted, and sure, some people call them and problems come up. But they know what to return to. Because they know their purpose. Because they chose it.

That's the kind of leader that is admired and followed.

23. See What's Possible

Outstanding leaders go out of the way to boost the self-esteem of their personnel. If people believe in themselves, it's amazing what they can accomplish.
—Sam Walton

One of the best ways to motivate others is to learn from those who have motivated *you*. Learn from the great leaders you have had. Channel them, clone them, and incorporate them into who you are all day.

⌘⌘⌘

Scott Richardson recalls: The most effective, inspirational motivator that I ever had was a violin prodigy who was my violin teacher. He was an associate professor of music at the University of Arizona named Rodney Mercado. I met him when I was 16 and ready to quit the violin. My mother, who desperately wanted me to be a violin player, said, "Hang on, I'll find you the best teacher out there."

I was skeptical. But one day, she came in and said to me, "I found him; he's the teacher of your teacher."

The first time I met him, I had to audition for him. I'd never had to audition for a teacher before. Usually you'd just pay the money, and they took you. But Mercado chose his students carefully, just as a great leader chooses his team.

And I gave the absolutely worst audition I'd ever given in my life! I thought, *Well, that sealed it. I don't have to worry about having him for my teacher.*

Soon after, he called me on the phone and said, "I've accepted you."

And I thought, *There must be some mistake, this can't be true. I mean, my playing was so horrible, I couldn't imagine anyone accepting me based on that.*

But he had the ability to see what was possible in other people. If anyone else had heard my audition, they would have said that it was hopeless. But he heard more than the playing. He heard the possibility behind the playing.

And in that, he was a profoundly great coach and leader, because one of the most vital aspects of motivating others is the ability to see what's possible instead of just seeing what's happening now.

Ever since that time, I've learned not to give up on people too quickly. I've learned to look deeply and listen deeply. Soon, skills and strengths I never saw before in people would show up.

I learned that people perform in response to who they think they are for us at the moment. In other words, how we see others is how they perform for us. Once we create a new possibility for those around us and communicate that to them, their performance as that person instantly takes off.

Professor Mercado showed me another example of the power of communicating possibility when he was teaching a boy named Michael, who later became a good friend of mine.

Michael was unusual. When he was in junior high, as far as I could guess, he had never ever cut his long black hair because it was longer than his sister's, which was down below her belt. And Michael always kept his hair in front of his face, so you actually couldn't see what he looked like. And he never spoke a word in public.

His parents asked Mr. Mercado if he would be willing to teach Michael the violin. Mr. Mercado agreed and they had lessons, but as far as any outsider could tell, it was strictly a one-way communication. Michael never responded outwardly. He never even picked up the violin!

Yet Mr. Mercado continued to teach him, week after week.

And then one day, when he was in 8th grade, Michael picked up the violin and started playing. And in less than a month, he was asked to solo in front of the Tucson Symphony!

I could see for myself that this happened because Mr. Mercado communicated to Michael (without any outward acknowledgment that communication was being received) that who Michael was for Mr. Mercado was a virtuoso violinist.

So I have always remembered from this experience that people's performance is a response to who they perceive themselves to be for us at the moment. Once we create a new possibility for those around us, and communicate to them that this new possibility is who they are for us, their performance instantly takes off.

⌘⌘⌘

There's no better way to motivate another human being.

24. Enjoy the A.R.T. of Confrontation

*To command is to serve, nothing more, and nothing
less. —André Malraux, French philosopher*

One of the tricks we teach to inspire increased motivation in others is what we call "The A.R.T. of Confrontation." It shows leaders how to enjoy holding people accountable.

Most managers think it's impossible to *enjoy* holding people accountable. They think it's the hard part of being a manager. They think it's one of the downsides—a necessary evil associated with the burden of command.

You can see why they don't do a very good job of holding people accountable.

Fortunately, there is an enjoyable way to do it.

When you need to speak to an employee about a behavior or a performance level that is not working for you, experiment with using A.R.T.:

A: First, appreciate and acknowledge the employee for who she is what she brings to the organization, noting specific strengths and talents. Then give a very *specific* recent example of something that employee did that particularly impressed and benefited you.

R: Next, restate your own commitment to that person. "I believe in you. I hired you because of what I saw in you. I see even more in you than when I hired you. I am committed to your success here. I am devoted to your career, to you being happy and fulfilled." Then, tell that employee exactly and specifically what she can count on, always, from you. List what you do, how you fight for fair pay, how you are available at all times, how you work to always get the employee the tools she needs for success, and so on.

This recommitment places the conversation in the proper context. Ninety percent of managerial "reprimands" are destructive to the manager-employee relationship because they are felt to be out of context. The big picture must be established first, always.

T: Last, track the agreement. You want to track the existing agreement you have with your employee (if there is one) about the matter in question. If there is no existing agreement, you should create one on the spot. Mutually authored with mutual respect. Agreements are cocreations. They are not mandates or rules. When an agreement is not being kept, both sides need to put all their cards on the table in a mutually supportive way to either rebuild the agreement or create a new agreement. People will break other people's rules. But people will keep their own agreements.

25. Feed Your Healthy Ego

Learning to be a leader is the same process as learning to be an integrated and healthy person.
—Warren Bennis

High self-esteem is our birthright. It is the core spirit inside of us. We do not need to pass a battery of humiliating tests to attain it. We need only to drop the thinking that contaminates it. We need to get out of its way and let it shine, in ourselves and in others.

Masterful, artful, spirited leadership has ways of bringing out the best and the highest expression of self-esteem in others.

But it starts at home. If I'm a leader, it starts with my own self-confidence. We human beings find it easier to follow self-confident people. We are quicker to become enrolled in a project when the person enrolling us is self-confident.

Most managers today don't take time to raise their own self-esteem and get centered in their personal pride of achievement. They spend too much time worrying about how they are being perceived, which results in insecurity and low self-esteem.

Nathaniel Branden, in his powerful book *Self Esteem at Work*, says it this way:

> A person who feels undeserving of achievement and success is unlikely to ignite high aspirations in others. Nor can leaders draw forth the best in others if their primary need, arising from their insecurities, is to prove themselves right and others wrong, in which case their relationship to others is not inspirational but adversarial. *It is a fallacy to say that a great leader should be egoless.* A leader needs an ego sufficiently healthy that it does not perceive itself as on trial in every encounter—is not operating out of anxiety and defensiveness—so that the leader is free to be task- and results-oriented, not oriented toward self-aggrandizement or self-protection. A healthy ego asks: What needs to be done? An insecure ego asks: How do I avoid looking bad?

Build your inner strength by doing what needs to be done and then moving to the next thing that needs to be done. The less you focus on how you're coming across, the better you'll come across.

26. Hire the Motivated

The best executive is the one who has sense enough to pick good people to do what he wants done, and self-restraint to keep from meddling with them while they do it. —Theodore Roosevelt

It sounds too simple. But the best way to have people on your team be motivated is to hire self-motivated people. There is much you can do to create this kind of team. Let's start with the hiring interview.

As you conduct your hiring interview, know in advance the kinds of questions that are likely to have been anticipated by the interviewee, and therefore will only get you a role-played answer. Minimize those questions.

Instead, ask questions that are original and designed to uncover the real person behind the role-player. Ask the unexpected. Keep your interviewee pleasantly off-balance. The good, motivated people will love it, and the under-motivated will become more and more uncomfortable.

Know that all interviewees are attempting to role-play. They are playing the part of the person they think would get this job. We all do it in an interview. But your job is to not let it happen.

One way to find the true person across from you is called *layering*. Layering is following up a question with an open-ended, layered addition to the question. For example:

Question: Why did you leave Company X?

Answer: Not enough challenges.

Layered Question: Interesting, tell me more about Company X. What was it like for you there?

Answer: It was pretty difficult. I wasn't comfortable.

Layered Question: Why do you think it affected you that way?

Answer: My manager was a micro-manager.

Layered Question: This is very interesting; talk more about that if you can.

Basically, layering is a request you are making that your interviewee "go on" and then "keep going" and then "tell me more."

Layering gets you the real person after a while. So do questions that have not been anticipated and rehearsed for a role-play. Here's an example of a very open-ended and curious exchange:

"Did you grow up here?"

"No, I grew up in Chicago."

"Chicago! Did you go to high school there?"

"Yes I did, Maine East High."

"What was that like, going to that school?"

Another example:

"How was your weekend?"

"Great."

"What is a typical weekend like for you?"

Or another:

"I see from your resume that you majored in engineering."

"Yes."

"If you had one thing to change about how they teach engineering, what would you change?"

Or another:

"If you were asked to go back to run the company you just came from, what's the first thing you would do?"

Think of questions that you yourself like and are intrigued by, and keep your interviewee in uncharted waters throughout the interview. That way you get the real person to talk to you so you'll get a much better feeling about what it would be like to work with him or her.

The best way to create a highly motivated team is to hire people who are already motivated.

27. Stop Talking

> One measure of leadership is the caliber of people
> who choose to follow you. —Dennis A. Peer,
> management consultant

Most job interviewers talk way too much...and they go way too soon to the question, "Well, is there anything you would like to know about us?"

Learn to stop doing that. That's your ego being expressed—not a good interview technique. People who have not done their homework and who are not masterful interviewers will always end up interviewing themselves and talking about their company.

They get uncomfortable asking lots of questions so they quickly start talking about the history of the company, their own history there, and many personal convictions and opinions. In this, they are wasting their time. In five months, they will be wringing their hands and tearing their hair out because somehow they let a problem employee and chronic complainer fly in under the radar.

Remember: no talking. Your job is to intuit the motivational level of the person across from you. You can only do that by letting her answer question after question.

It takes more courage, imagination, and preparation to ask a relentless number of questions than it does to chat. But great leaders are great recruiters. In sports and in life. As a leader, you're only as good as your people. Hire the best.

Dale Dauten, often called the Obi-Wan Kenobi of business consultants, said, "When I did the research that led to my book *The Gifted Boss*, I found that great bosses spend little time trying to mold employees into greatness, but instead devote extraordinary efforts to spotting and courting exceptionally capable employees. Turns out that the best management is finding employees that don't need managing."

28. Refuse to Buy Their Limitation

> Leaders don't create followers, they create more leaders. —Tom Peters

Your people limit themselves all the time. They put up false barriers and struggle with imaginary problems.

One of your skills as a leader is to show your people that they can accomplish more than they think they can. In fact, they may someday be leaders like you. And one of the reasons your people wind up admiring you is that you always see their potential. You always see the best side of them, and you tell them about it.

It could be that you are the first person in that employee's life to *ever* believe in him. And because of you, he becomes more capable than he thought he was, and he loves you for that, even though your belief in him sometimes makes him uncomfortable. That discomfort may return every time you ask him to stretch. But you don't care. You press on with your belief in him, stretching him, growing him.

One of the greatest leadership gurus of American business was Robert Greenleaf. He developed the concept of "servant leadership." A leader is one who serves those following, serving them every step of the way, especially by bringing out the best in them and *refusing to* buy their limitations as achievers.

Your people may be flawed as people, but as achievers, they are certainly not.

Greenleaf said, "Anybody could lead perfect people—if there were any. But there aren't any perfect people. And parents who try to raise perfect children are certain to raise neurotics.

"It is part of the enigma of human nature that the 'typical' person—immature, stumbling, inept, lazy—is capable of great dedication and heroism if wisely led. The secret of team-building is to be able to weld a team of such people by lifting them up to grow taller than they would otherwise be."

29. Play Both Good Cop and Bad Cop

If your actions inspire others to dream more, learn more, do more, and become more, you are a leader.
—John Quincy Adams

If you are an effective motivator of others, then you know how to play good cop/bad cop. And you know that you don't need two people to play it. A true motivator plays both roles.

Good cop: Nurturing, mentoring, coaching, serving, and supporting your people all the way. Keeping your word every time. Removing obstacles to success. Praising and acknowledging all the way. Leading through positive reinforcement of desired behavior, because you're a true leader who knows that you get what you reward.

Bad cop: Bad to the bone. No compromise about people keeping their promises to you, even promises about performance. No complaints and excuses as substitutions for conversations about promises not being kept. No respect for whiners and people who do not make their numbers. No "wiggle room" for the lazy. Clarity, conviction, determination. All cards on the table. No covert messages. In your face: "I believe in you. I know what you can do. The whole reason you exist here, in my life, is to get this job done."

Obviously you don't call on bad cop very often. Only after every good cop approach is exhausted. Bad cop can be a great wake-up call to someone who has never been challenged in life to be the best she can be. And once the bad cop session is over and the person is back in the game, giving it a good effort, bring good cop back right away to complete the process.

30. Don't Go Crazy

> The older I get the more wisdom I find in the ancient
> rule of taking first things first. A process which often
> reduces the most complex human
> problem to a manageable proportion.
> —Dwight D. Eisenhower

When I'm thinking about seven things rather than one, I'm trying to keep them in my head and I'm trying to listen to you, but I really can't because I just thought of three more things that I need to attend to when you leave, which I hope will be soon.

So I look at my watch a couple of times while you're talking to me, because mentally I'm on the run, and I'm a type-A guy, doing a million things, but what I'm not seeing is that my very fragile relationship with you is being destroyed by this approach. It's being destroyed a little bit at a time., because the main message I'm sending to you and everyone else on my team is that I'm really stressed, *and it's crazy here.*

I even tell my family, "It's crazy here. I want to spend more time with you, but it's crazy right now. Just crazy at the office."

Well, it's not crazy. *You're* crazy. You need to be honest about it. *It's* not crazy, it's just work. It's just a business.

It's-crazy-around-here managers keep throwing up their hands, saying, "What? She's leaving us? Why? She's quitting? Oh no, you can't trust anybody these days. Get her in here, we need to save this. Cancel my meetings, cancel my calls, I want to find out why she's leaving."

Well, she's leaving for this reason: You only spoke to her for a maximum of three minutes in any single conversation during the past year. You may have spoken to her 365 times, but it was only for three minutes. This is not a professional relationship. It's a drive-by shooting.

Whether the manager likes it or not, creating great relationships is how careers are built, how businesses are built, and how great teams are built.

Usually people who admire or in a certain, frightened, way "respect" their multitasking managers, admit that they feel less secure because of all that is "crazy." When they meet with the manager, the manager says to them, "Okay, come on in, I know you need to see me. Get in here, I have to take this call. It's crazy. I've got to be in a meeting in two minutes, and there's an e-mail I'm waiting for, so you'll forgive me if I jump on that when it comes in, but just step in here for a second. I know you had something on your mind. So please, ah, talk to me...oh excuse me."

When we can get managers to experiment with slowing down and becoming focused on each conversation as a way to approach their day, they're really amazed. If they do it for a week, they call back and say, "Unbelievably, I got more understanding of my people this week than in all my previous weeks on this job."

It's unbelievable to them. Because often, when they slow down and look at the next urgent task in front of them, it occurs to them that *someone else would love to do this task.* Not only that, but someone else would be *flattered* to do this. "They would enjoy hearing about the trust I have in them by asking them to take this over and get it done, and done well, because I like the way they do things."

There are so many things that can be delegated and passed on to others, but only if you regain your sanity and slow down.

One of the best ways to motivate others is to give them more interesting things to do, especially things that free your own time up. That's time you can use to build a motivated team.

31. Stop Cuddling Up

> I never gave them hell. I just tell the truth and they think it's hell. —Harry Truman

Unconsciously, managers without leadership habits will often seek, above all else, to be liked. Rather than holding people accountable, they let them off the hook. They give nonperformers the uneasy feeling that everything's fine. They are managers who seek approval rather than respect. But this habit has a severe consequence. It leads to a lack of trust in the workplace, the most common "issue" cited on employee surveys.

A true leader does not focus first on trying to be liked. A true leader focuses on the practices and communications that lead to being *respected*. It's a completely different goal that leads to completely different results. (I am not motivated by you because I like you; I am motivated by you because I respect you.)

The core internal question that the leader returns to is, "If I were being managed by me, what would I most need from my leader right now?"

The answer to that question varies, but most often comes up as:

1. The truth, as soon as you know the truth.
2. Full and complete communication about what's going on with me and with us.

3. Keeping all promises, especially the small ones ("I'll get back to you by tomorrow with that") consistently, even fanatically. Not some promises, not a high percentage of promises, not a good college try, but all promises. When a promise cannot be kept (especially a small one), an immediate apology, update, and new promise is issued.

A true leader does not try to become everybody's big buddy, although he or she values being upbeat and cheerful in communication. A true leader is not overly concerned with always being liked, and is even willing to engage in very uncomfortable conversations in the name of being straight and thorough. A true leader sees this aspect of leadership in very serious, adult terms and does not try to downplay responsibility for leadership. True leaders do not try to form inappropriate private friendships with members of the team they are paid to lead. A true leader enjoys all the elements of accountability and responsibility and transforms performance measurement and management into an aboveboard business adventure.

32. Do the Worst First

> The best way out is always through.
> —Robert Frost

The number-one topic that leaders ask us to speak about these days is: How do you motivate others when you have poor time-management? This was true of Carlos who headed up a team of brokers.

"With everything that's flying at me, everything that's coming in, all the calls that I get, all the obligations that I have, everything that there is to do in a given day, I could really use another 10 hours in my day," Carlos said.

We laughed: "This is true of everyone, Carlos. Stop thinking you are unique. Reprogram and bring yourself into focus. Reboot your mind. Start over."

All functional people in this global market have more to do than they have time to do. That's not really a problem. It's an exciting fact of life.

"But it's very, very tempting to cave in to a sense of being overwhelmed," Carlos said. "It's tempting to get into that victim mindset of being 'swamped.'"

"True enough. So regroup and get the view from 10,000 feet. Rise up. Lift yourself up!"

"But the truth is, I *am* swamped," Carlos almost yelled out. "There's nothing I can do. I'm overwhelmed. How can anyone manage this team when you've got all this stuff going on? And right when you think you're getting ahead of it, you get a call, you get an e-mail, you get another request, there's another program that has to be implemented, there's another form that has to be filled out, and I'm about to throw up my hands and say, 'How do I do this?'"

"Carlos, listen. Get a grip for now. The simplest system that you can come up with for time-management will serve you as a leader. Keep it simple."

"Why does it have to be simple?" Carlos asked. "It seems like I need a more complex solution to a complex set of challenges."

"Because no matter what you do, you can't stop this one truth about leadership: You are going to be hounded, you're going to be barraged, and you're going to be interrupted. And there are two reactions you can choose between to address this leadership fact of life."

Carlos said nothing.

"You could just become a victim and say, 'I can't handle it, there's just too much to do.' That takes no imagination, it takes no courage, and it's simply the easiest way to go—to complain about your situation. Maybe even complain to other people, other leaders, other managers, other family members; they will all shake their heads, and finally they will say, 'You've got to get out of that business.'"

Carlos started nodding in agreement.

"That happens," Carlos said. "But that doesn't help me enjoy my job: to have friends and family feeding back to me that I ought to get out of the business. That makes it twice as hard."

"Right! So there's another way to go, and this is by keeping the simplest time-management system possible in your life. This is the one that we recommend, and it's the one that most leaders have had the most luck with. It's so simple, you can boil it down to two words, if you have to. The words are: *Worst first!*"

We worked with Carlos for a long time to get him to see that the best way to manage his time is not to think of it as managing time, but to think of it as managing *priorities*. Because you can't really "manage time." You can't add any more time to your day.

But you *can* manage the priorities and the things that you choose to do.

"Worst first," Carlos said. "What does that mean?"

"Put on a piece of paper all the things you'd like to do in the upcoming day. Maybe you've been jotting them down the last couple of days, but these are things that you know you would like to do. The list doesn't have to be perfect. It can be all kinds of shorthand, and little pictures and drawings, all over a scratched up piece of paper. Then you *choose*, among all these things, the one thing that's the most challenging and important."

"How do I know for sure what that is? And how will this, in the long run, improve the motivation of my people? Isn't that your area of specialty?"

"Yes, it is, but until you get this down, you can't motivate anyone. You have to have a solid place to come from, an organized place inside yourself."

"Okay, okay, I know that, but how do I choose the one thing to focus on?"

"What is that *one thing* that you're most likely to put off? What's the most important thing to do, the thing that really needs to be done; not necessarily the most urgent thing, but the most important?"

"Oh," said Carlos, "I think I'm seeing this. That thing that pains me most to think of. That's what I select to do first."

"That's it."

Most managers are like Carlos. They don't have a simple system. They just respond to whatever's most urgent. All day they wonder, "What absolutely has to be addressed right now?" And a lot of time, the urgent things that come up as answers to that question are really small. They're nitpicky things, just hassles.

"But don't the little things have to be done?" Carlos asked.

"Yeah, they have to be done, but in the meantime, you're leaving important things behind. Many times, it is even more effective to turn off your phones, get away from your e-mail, select something that's important, do that until it's complete, and let the urgent go hang."

"I do know that there's always something that eats at the back of my mind," Carlos said. "It keeps coming up, I keep thinking about it. It gets in the way of the things I'm doing."

"Now you're on the right track, Carlos! You can't focus in a relaxed and cheerful way on the things you are doing because in the back of your mind, this important thing is there. When you go home at night, the thing that makes you the most weary, the most under-the-weather, and most gives you the sense of not having had a good day, is that one thing you didn't do, but you wish you had."

"Right. Boy, do I know."

"So you want to get into the category of Worst First: You want to pick that one thing that's hardest to do, that you would love to have finished and behind you. You want to make it *number one*. First priority. Nothing gets done until that gets done."

Weeks went by, and Carlos struggled with the system, but finally warmed up to it after a lot of practice. After Carlos had finally made the "worst first" system into a habit, he felt a freedom he never felt before. People around him were inspired by how liberated he was every day from having done the hardest thing first. Carlos would handle his biggest thing as his first thing, and then live like the rest of the day was a piece of cake. His energy soared. Soon he was teaching others the same system.

He called a few months later to give an update on his newly centered life in leadership.

"I am really freed up by this," Carlos said. "If someone says to me, 'Will you sit down and talk to me about this issue?' and I have done my worst thing already, I can say 'Sure, how much time do you need? Let's talk.'"

33. Learn to Experiment

> Don't be too timid and squeamish about your
> actions. All life is an experiment. The more
> experiments you make, the better.
> —Ralph Waldo Emerson

One of the most common complaints of today's executives is this: The people they supervise hate to make changes though they are constantly being required to in this highly competitive business environment. The executives then tear out their hair trying to get the needed changes implemented.

The way we respond is that it may feel difficult to encourage people to change. But try this possibility: People may prefer not to change, but people love to experiment. As business consultant and journalist Dale Dauten has observed, "Experimentation never fails. When you try something and it turns out to be a lousy idea, you never really go back to where you started. You learned something. If nothing else, it makes you appreciate what you were doing before. So I think it's true that experiments never fail."

So in the businesses that we coach, there are never any changes. However, our clients' businesses are constantly *experimenting* to find what works better for the employees, the business, and the customer. The executives simply tell their teams, "This is an experiment to see if it works better for you and our customers. If it does, great, we are going to continue doing it. If it doesn't, then we will modify it or get rid of it."

And as long as you monitor it and get feedback, you'll find that the old-fashioned resistance to change melts away because your employees really do enjoy a good experiment.

34. Communicate Consciously

> Drowning in data, yet starved of information.
> —Ruth Stanat, global business consultant

Communicate consciously. Be aware of how you are being heard.

Leadership authority Warren Bennis says, "Good leaders make people feel that they're at the very heart of things, not at the periphery. Everyone feels that he or she makes a difference to the success of the organization. When that happens people feel centered and that gives their work meaning."

We live in the information age. Your people use their minds creatively and productively throughout the day. They aren't in some ditch just shoveling dirt. They all communicate for a living. Now more than ever before, communication is our lifeblood. It is the lifeblood of every organization. Yet, many organizations leave most of their communication to chance, or to "common sense," or to old traditions that no longer function to keep everyone informed and included.

Communication is the source of trust and respect within each organization. So let's put all our cards on the table as often as possible.

When we increase our awareness of communication, communication is enhanced. When we take full responsibility for how we communicate, the organization is enhanced.

35. Score the Performance

Performance is your reality. Forget everything else.
—Harold Geneen, CEO, ITT

Can you imagine playing a game in which you don't know how it's scored, or competing in front of judges, but you don't know their criteria? And the judges are not going to tell you for a long time how you did. That would be a nightmare.

We sat in a meeting run by Megan, who was having a hard time motivating her team to hit the company's expected goals.

"Exactly how are we doing right now?" her team member Clarence asked Megan from the end of the round table around which we were all sitting.

"Oh, I don't know, Clarence," said Megan. "I haven't looked at the printout yet. I have a sense that we are doing pretty well this month, but I haven't gotten to the numbers yet."

You could see the look on Clarence's face. It was a cross between disappointment and pain.

Later, we met with Megan alone and explained to her why she needed to change her approach immediately if she had any hope of motivating Clarence and his teammates. She had to know the score.

"I just don't enjoy numbers," Megan said. "I never have. I'm not a numbers kind of person."

"Whether you enjoy numbers or not, if you're in a leadership position, it is imperative to be *the* numbers person for your team. There's no way you're going to have a motivated team here, Megan, until you do your homework, put the numbers in front of you, and *talk about those numbers* when you talk to your people. If you're their coach, and you are, then you talk about the game and the score."

"Well, I played a little basketball in high school," Megan said. "Maybe I can relate it to that."

"Imagine your basketball coach during a game. Your team comes to the sideline, it's late in the game, and your coach says, 'Now, I haven't looked at the scoreboard for a while, so I don't know how many points we're down, or are we up? Anyway, here are some plays that I think we ought to run after the time-out.'"

Megan smiled and said, "That would be a coach that I wouldn't have any confidence in whatsoever!"

"Why not?"

Megan said nothing.

"Aren't you that coach, Megan?"

Megan said, "I think I see what you mean. My best coaches were people who rewarded numbers and got excited."

"Right! Great leaders are the same. They are leaders who call team members and say, 'Hey, I just got your numbers for last week. Wow, that's better than you've done all year!' These are the leaders people love to follow, because they always know whether they are winning or losing. They always know the score."

We reminded Megan that earlier in her team meeting she had said to her group, "Well, you guys are really trying hard and I know you are making the effort. I drove by last night and I saw your lights on late, so I really admire what you guys are doing. You're really giving it the old college try." We told her that she might be on the wrong course with that approach.

"What was wrong with saying that?" Megan asked.

"It's wrong because respect for achievement is replaced by respect for 'trying.' Megan, listen, we have a phrase in our society's language that sums it up. When someone is willfully dense and ineffective, we say that person doesn't know the score.' Why? Because 'knowing the score' is the first step in all achievement."

What we wanted Megan to see was that this mistake of hers was immediately correctable. It was only the mistake of not looking over some numbers before sending an e-mail or making a call.

But that one little mistake will give a leader's team the impression that they're there for reasons other than winning and achieving precise goals.

The coach has to be the one to explain to the team with tremendous precision exactly what the score is, exactly how much time is left, and exactly what the strategy is based on those numbers. When you have a numbers-based team, you know when you are winning, you know when you've had a good day, you know when you're having a good run, and you know when you are not.

That creates a wonderful sense that there is no hidden agenda from this leader. So look for ways, as you communicate with your people, to improve and increase the way they are measured, and especially to increase the consciousness of that measurement.

But it has to come from you. You can't wait around for the company policy to shift. That's what most people do. They wait for their own management to come up with some kind of new system, new scorebooks, new posters, something like that. But don't do that. Don't wait. Have it come from you.

It has to be *your personal innovation* to find more ways to keep score. That way, people will link it to you and know how much it means to you. Is there anything that you want improved? Find ways to track it, to keep score of it. The love of games that is in every human being is something that you can tap into. The more you measure things, the more motivated your people are to do those measured things.

36. Manage the Fundamentals First

Show me a man who cannot bother to do little things and I'll show you a man who cannot be trusted to do big things.
—Lawrence D. Bell, founder, Bell Aircraft

The Rodney Mercado motivational methods are not only the most effective methods for teaching music, but for anything else. Mercado was a genius in 10 different fields, including mathematics, economics, sociology, anthropology, and music history.

⌘⌘⌘

Scott recalls: Once, I was surprised to be getting an economics lesson inside my music lesson. Mercado turned to me and said, "Well, Scott, you know, math is very, very simple. It's all based on addition. But most people lose sight of that. So if you learn how to do one plus one equals two, everything in math flows from that. Everything."

He was always focusing on fundamentals. Like the time he came to assist our chamber group in preparing to perform a piece. Under his guidance, we spent the entire hour working on the first two measures of this piece. We kept going over and over them, and each time he would ask us to explore a new possibility.

"How would you like to create more sound here?" he would ask. And then he would give us ideas on how we might possibly do that. And by the end of the hour, all we had done was work on two measures of a piece that probably had 80 measures of music. Then, at the very end, he said, "Okay, now let's play the whole thing." The entire performance and our entire group were transformed. We played the whole thing beautifully! That showed me the power of fundamentals. Don't gloss over them. Slow your people down and do things step by step, getting the basics right, getting the fundamentals in place.

⌘⌘⌘

We coached a client in his company-wide managers' meeting, and two people didn't show up on time for the meeting. The CEO wanted to rush through the meeting and "talk to the people who didn't show up" later.

But we slowed him down and had the whole group focus, slowly and fundamentally, on how to handle this tardiness and absenteeism and lack of commitment from these two managers. In the process, we had a number of breakthrough moments for other managers on the nature of commitment, and a newer, more creative policy emerged.

37. Motivate by Doing

People can be divided into two classes: those who go ahead and do something, and those people who sit still and inquire, why wasn't it done the other way?
—Oliver Wendell Holmes

Most managers don't do things in the order of a priority that they've rationally selected. They do things according to feelings. That's how their day is run. (This, by the way, is exactly how infants live. They live from feeling to feeling. Do they feel like crying? Do they feel like laughing? Do they feel like drooling? That's an infant's life.)

Professional managers fall into one of two categories. There are doers and there are feelers. Doers do what needs to be done to reach a goal that they themselves have set. They come to work having planned out what needs to be done. Feelers, on the other hand, do what they feel like doing. Feelers take their emotional temperature throughout the day, checking in on themselves, figuring out what they feel like doing right now. Their lives, their outcomes, their financial security are all dictated by the fluctuation of their feelings. Their feelings will change constantly, of course, so it's hard for a feeler to follow anything through to a successful conclusion. Their feelings are changed by many things: biorhythms, gastric upset, a strong cup of coffee, an annoying call from home, a rude waitress at lunch, a cold, a bit of a headache. Those are the dictating forces, the commanders, of a feeler's life.

A doer already knows in advance how much time will be spent on the phone, how much in the field, what employees will be cultivated that day, what relationships will be strengthened, what communications need to be made. Doers use a three-step system to guaranteed success:

1. They figure out what they want to achieve.
2. They figure out what needs to be done to achieve it.
3. They just do it.

This is not a theory—this is the actual observed system used by all super achievers without fail.

A feeler is adrift in a mysterious life of unexpected consequences and depressing problems. A feeler asks, "Do I feel like making my phone calls now?" "Do I feel like writing that thank you note?" "Do I feel like dropping in on that person right now?" If the answer is no, then the feeler keeps going down the list, asking, "Do I feel like doing something else?" A feeler lives inside that line of inquiry all day long.

By contrast, a doer has high self-esteem. A doer enjoys many satisfactions throughout the day, even though some of them were preceded by discomfort. A feeler is almost always comfortable, but never really satisfied. A doer knows the true, deep joy that only life's super achievers know. A feeler believes that joy is for children, and that life for an adult is an ongoing hassle. A doer experiences more and more power every year of life. A feeler feels less and less powerful as the years go on.

Your ability to motivate others increases exponentially as your reputation as a *doer* increases. You also get more and more clarity about who the doers and feelers are on your own team. Then, as you model and reward the doing, you also begin to inspire the feelers on your team to be doers.

38. Know Your People's Strengths

Those few who use their strengths to incorporate
their weaknesses, who don't divide themselves, those
people are very rare. In any generation there are a few
and they lead their generation.
—Moshe Feldenkrais, psychologist

Know your people's strengths.

It's the fundamental business insight that inspired the
book *From Good to Great* by Jim Collins. And this idea of going from good to great also applies to the people you motivate.
It's far more effective to build on their strengths than to worry
too much about their weaknesses. The first step is to really
know their strengths so you can help them to express them
even more.

Most managers spend way too much time, especially in
the world of sales, trying to fix what's wrong. Your people
may identify negative things and say, "Oh, I'm not good at
this. I need to change that. And I'm not very good on the
phone. I need to fix that...." But listen to their voice tones
when they say these things! They'll always sound depressed
and world-weary.

Here's the simple formula (and once we recognize this
formula, we can do some wonderful things): If people focus
on what's wrong with them, *just focusing on that* puts them
in a bad mood. People grimly and glumly confront what's
wrong with a kind of morbid honesty. The voice tone goes
down, because the enthusiasm goes down, and the dreariness
sets in. And pretty soon, they're putting off activities. They're
procrastinating. They're saying, "This makes me uncomfortable. I don't even like thinking about this right now. For some

reason (I don't know why), I was in a good mood before I started.... I'm not in the mood to work on this. I can tell that I can't work on this problem until I feel a little more energy. I mean, you can't work on something when there's no energy to work."

We went into a computer company and listened as the manager, Matt, talked about his team.

"I wish my salespeople would do more research before their sales calls," Matt said.

And then when we sat down with one of Matt's salespeople, Byron, he said, "Yeah, that's something I'm not very good at."

"Okay, you're not very good at that. So let's move on."

"No, no, I need to fix that," said Byron. "That's something that needs to be fixed. I need to get better. Why don't you coach me? How do I get better at that?"

And we could hear his low voice tone. We knew Byron would never get better at that. Because of the negative mindset the very subject put him in.

To really take something on and to grow and strengthen it, people need to be in an upbeat, positive mood. People need to have energy. That's when they're at their best.

"So, when will my people have energy?" manager Matt asked us after we explained the concept of moods to him.

"They get energy when they think about the things they're really good at in sales. Have them ask themselves, 'What am I really good at? What are my strengths?' The minute they start focusing on those things, their energy will pick up. Their self-esteem will pick up. Their enthusiasm will pick up."

That's where the fastest infusion of productivity always comes from. First, you find what this person is good at, and then you move good to great.

When we worked with Byron we said, "Okay, Byron, forget about your weaknesses, forget about what you're not good at. That's probably all you've been thinking about for a few months, right?"

"Right," said Byron. "You know, my manager counsels me on it. I've had things written up about it. I've been given activities to do to correct it. But the problem is, I'm not in the energetic level I need to be in to do anything with it, so I just go deeper, and I don't produce."

"Listen, Byron, set those activities aside. Forget about all the problems that need to be fixed. We're not going to fix anything for now. We want an infusion, we want a stimulus. We want a burst of sales to take you out of the cellar and put you up there where you belong in the upper rankings of the salespeople. Later, when we have the luxury, and we're bored, and we can't figure out what to do in coaching session, we may take a weakness and play around with it, for the pure fun of it. But for now, we're not going to do it. Here's what we're going to do. We're going to acknowledge one thing: *You're not going to be great at anything until you enjoy it.* We want to find out what you're already good at, and we want to build on that."

"Well, one of my strengths is in-person," said Byron. "I love to be in-person. I'm bad on the phone, I'm bad with faxes, I'm bad with e-mail. But in-person, I can just close deals, I can talk, I can expand, I can upsell, I can cross-sell...."

"Okay, great. So rather than fix the phone thing and fix the e-mail thing, let's leave those aside for the moment. Only use them if you must to get an appointment. Don't use them to sell anything. We want to increase what you're good at. Get out there, sit with people. Keep increasing that and get even better at it. Don't say 'I'm already good at it, and that's that.' Of course you're good at it. But the way you're going to be really tremendous in this field is to turn good into great, to get *great* at that thing, because you're more than two-thirds of the way there. Because you're already good at it."

What we wanted to steer Byron away from is this thought: *Well, I'm already good at it, that's sort of natural, that comes easy to me. That's sort of cheating when I do a lot of that. What I really need to do is work at what I'm bad at.*

To be great motivators, we need to look at human behavior differently. We've been taught the wrong way since we were young! If we got an "A" in science, but we flunked English, our parents said, "Hey, I don't care about your other grades, what you really need to do is work hard on your English, because you flunked it. So you're going to focus your life on English for a while."

All of our lives, we've been taught that the way to succeed is to take something that we're not good at and change it. Take your weaknesses and spend time with them so that you can bring your weaknesses up to "normal."

Do you know how *little* an effect it has on someone's productivity if they take their weaknesses and work hard and finally bring them from "subnormal" to "normal"? All throughout life we've been taught that when we're good at something, it just means it's innate. Our parents say, "Oh, he's really good at the piano. He must have gotten that from his grandfather, he must have inherited that, he's got a natural talent at that." So we're taught not to focus on it. We're taught that that will be okay by itself. People tell us, "You *really* need to put your attention on all the things you're *bad* at!"

Jennifer was on a sales staff we were coaching, and she was kind of intimidated because the sales staff had a lot of flashy, good looking, well-dressed men and women on it. Jennifer was more of a shy person. She was very bright and very compassionate, but she just couldn't make herself do things the way the other salespeople did. And so she was frustrated, and all she tried to do was work on her weaknesses, and whenever we met her, she would bring in this long list of things she wasn't any good at.

"These are the things I want to talk about," Jennifer said. "These are the things, the top seven things I suck at, I'm terrible at."

"Throw that list out."

"What?"

"We don't care about that list. We really don't. You wouldn't be here if you didn't have the basic skills to be here. So stop it. Here's what we'd like you to do. Think back for a little while. Think about your life. When were you really happy? If you can look back and get in touch with moments in your life when you were really happy, it's going to give us some clues about where to go from here."

"Well, I was a waitress not too long ago, before I came here," Jennifer said. "There was a restaurant that I worked in that, originally, I didn't like, but finally just loved. I really enjoyed it. It was like I was in heaven, I just got so good at it. I was serving customers and I was taking their orders and I got the biggest tips of anybody there. It was just wonderful. It felt like a dance, it felt like a musical. And also, the money coming in to me was greater than it was for anyone else there."

"We've hit on something here!"

"Well, I can't do that." Jennifer said. "I've got bills to pay, I've got kids. I can't go back to that. There's not enough money there, no matter how good you are. I've got to do this. I've got to get the big accounts. I've got to get the big commissions I know I can make."

"So we're going to do that. But we're not going to do it from being a back-slapping, flashy salesperson. We're going to go with your strength."

"Well, my strength is waiting on tables and serving people."

"Yes! So that's what you're going to do. That's who you're going to be. You're going to serve. You're going to take orders. You're going to present menus. You're going to explain what the dishes are like. You're going to ask clients what they like. You're going to give them options, and that same person you were in the restaurant, you're going to be in this selling situation. You're going to tap into that same love of serving and presenting options and fulfilling orders. That's going to be who you are, but you're going to do it in this context, selling this product. And when you get on the phone, you're going to be that way, you're going to be the person who wants to know how you can help. Not a salesperson. Not a salesperson at all. You will use all the words you used when you were a happy waitress. 'You're not quite ready? I'd be glad to come back. Take your time. I want you to know what's here. I want you to know what the specials are, so you can make your decision.' And come from that point of view. That's who you are. That's a way of being that you loved. And you can be that here. You can serve rather than sell, and it will work for you."

Two or three months later, Jennifer was doing extremely well. She had made a remarkable breakthrough. She came at the job from a completely different place. She took what she loved to do the most, and she did *that* all day. She took what she already knew she was good at, she took a strength, and she moved it from good to great.

39. Debate Yourself

I am more afraid of an army of 100 sheep led by a lion than an army of 100 lions led by a sheep. —Talleyrand

All it might take is half a day to catch everything up, sort everything out, clean everything away, and be ready to begin next week with a whole new lease on life, staying organized as you go.

But still you resist.

You know you will never find time to do that half a day of reorganization. Therefore, you must *make* time. Winners make time to do what's really beneficial and important to them. Losers keep trying to find time.

When you hear a pessimistic manager say, "I'm sorry I didn't get back to you, Dave, I was swamped yesterday," that swamped feeling has become reality. But being swamped is just an interpretation. If that manager was locked in solitary confinement for five years, and somebody offered him this job in which he had a lot of phone calls and things to do, would he call it "being swamped"? He would call it being wonderfully busy. He would call it absolute heaven.

So which is it? Swamped or busy?

A woman in one of our workshops a year ago said, "My job is a total nightmare. It is hell on earth. The fact that I even show up for it is surprising to me—it is an absolute nightmare."

"What is the nightmare?"

"Well, I've got people calling in, I've got two different bosses, both telling me what to do. I've got an inbox stacked like this high, and I go home from work stressed out."

"Okay, what if we were to introduce you to a woman from Nigeria whose husband has been dead for two years and who has had to eat out of garbage cans to live—do you think you could persuade her that your job is a nightmare? Would she like trading lives with you? Would your job be a nightmare to that woman?"

"Oh, no, not to her it wouldn't be a nightmare. It would be the greatest blessing."

"So, is your job a nightmare? A nightmare is only a nightmare in your own thinking. It's a perception. You can choose another if you want. You can choose another job, or you can choose another perception. You are free."

Be willing to teach your people how to debate themselves. When we question our own thinking, we start to elevate to new levels of thinking. We start to really accomplish things if we have enough courage to question our own thinking. Here are some questions we might want to ask ourselves, for beginners: "Is that really true? Is my manager really out to get me? Is this really happening? Is this really a bad opportunity? It might be, but is it really? What else could I say about it? What would be a more useful way to interpret it?" We can teach people to question everything negative.

Be ruthless with yourself, too, as you debate the chaos that builds up in your life. Simplify your life to feel your full power. When Vince Lombardi was asked why his world-champion football team had the simplest offensive system in all of football, his response was, "It's hard to be aggressive when you're confused."

40. Lead With Language

The first responsibility of a leader is to define reality.
—Max DePree, business consultant and author

We once worked with a group of managers who managed various teams in a company plagued with low morale. The teams were grumbling and exulting in victim language. But once we suggested different words and language for the managers to use in team meetings, everything began to change. Their people became more self-motivated.

As the psychological turnaround advanced, the managers began to open their meetings by asking who had an acknowledgement, "Who would like to acknowledge someone else right now?" and the talk began to swing to appreciation, instead of to complaint and criticism. And all of a sudden, the mood of the meetings changed. Instead of focusing on problems, and getting stuck there, the leaders would learn to say, "What opportunities do you see?" And just by saying that enough times, a different kind of energy would emerge, different than the low-morale days when the leaders used to say, "What are the problems? What do we have to get through? Who's to blame?"

When managers asked, "What can we get from this?" results changed faster.

"We had a tough week last week. Let's go around the table. What can we learn from that? What are some new systems we might put in? If that comes up again, what would be a great way of dealing with it? How can we have fun with this in the future?"

The managers got the victim language out of their systems. They became stronger by asking, "What do we want? What's our intention? What's our goal? What outcome would we love to see?" Every time victim language was replaced by the language of intention, different results occurred. Some of the most dramatic results:

1. Turnover decreased.

2. Absenteeism decreased.

3. Spirit and morale improved.

4. Productivity increased.

And that all happened with language.

Words mean things. Words that form thoughts create things. Ancient scriptures read, "In the beginning, there was the word." And there's a lot of modern-day truth to that. Words get things going. Change a single word in what you say, and you can scare a child to death. One scary word can make a child shake and cry. Change that word back, and the child is fine. Words communicate pictures, energy, emotions, possibilities, and fears. Words can scare an employee, too.

Sometimes victims try to be leaders, but can't. That's because they think they ought to do it. But the leadership spirit is not accessed that way. It's a graceful spirit, not a heavy burden. This won't get you there: "I *should* be more of a leader."

Any time a victim finds out about leadership language, and then says, "You know, I really should be more of a leader," that's simply more victim language! That drives the person deeper down into victim feelings.

Why should you be more of a leader?

"Well, I guess people would like me more. They would approve of me more."

Who cares what other people think? What do *you* want?

Leadership is based on personal, internal intention. It's living a life that has clarity of purpose at the center of it. Victimization is not based on intention. Victimization is based on being a victim of circumstance and other people's opinion. The victim is constantly obsessed with what other people think.

"Well, what would my wife think if I did that? What would my kids think? What would my boss think? What would the people think if they saw me singing in my car? If a person pulls up next to me, what's he gonna think?"

Obsessing about what other people think throughout the day is the fastest way to lose your enthusiasm for life. It's the fastest way to lose that basic energy that gets everything done that you've ever been proud of. You notice that children don't seem to have that worry. Most children, when they're in the middle of something they really love, seem to forget that anybody is watching them, and even forget that there's a world out there. They just get swept away. Good leaders do the same thing.

41. Use Positive Reinforcement

The first duty of a leader is optimism. How does your subordinate feel after meeting with you? Does he feel uplifted? If not, you are not a leader.
—Field Marshall Montgomery

Nobody remembers it. Everybody seems to forget it. But positive reinforcement trumps negative criticism every time.

Why can't we remember that?

We're too busy chasing down problems and then criticizing the problem people who created the problems. That's how most managers "lead."

But that's a habit trap. And like any other habit trap, there are certain small behaviors that will remove you from that trap. For example, you will want to pause a moment before e-mailing or calling any of your team players. You will want to take a moment. You want to decide what small appreciation you can communicate to them. You will want to always realize that positive reinforcement is powerful when it comes to guiding and shaping human performance. This revelation continues to surprise us, because we have been trained by our society to identify what's wrong and fix it.

A very surprised Napoleon once said, "The most amazing thing I have learned about war is that men will die for ribbons."

42. Teach Your People "No" Power

As we look ahead into the next century, leaders will be those who empower others. —Bill Gates

The tragedy of the disempowered life extends to all aspects of work, unless you change it.

Tina reports to you. And one of the things she reports to you is that she is stressed and incapable of doing all of her work. After a long talk about her life on the job, it becomes clear that Tina has no goals, plans, or commitments. It is no wonder, therefore, that people feel free to waste Tina's time. People whom Tina doesn't even care about are taking all her time. She can't say no to them only because she hasn't said yes to anything else.

You talk to her. "The greatest value of planning and goal-setting is that it gives you your own life to live. It puts you back in charge. It allows you to focus on what's most important to you. So you won't walk around all week singing the Broadway song, 'I'm Just a Girl Who Can't Say No.'"

You begin to sing that song to her. She begs you to stop.

"Okay, how do I turn it around?" Tina asks you. "How do I learn to say no?"

"Ask yourself these questions: 'What goals are most important to me? How much time do I give them? Which people are most important to me? And how much time do I give them?'"

We hear many complaints from people in business who are going through the same kind of scattered lives. It's as if they're dying from a thousand tiny distractions. They report a life of being constantly drained by other people's requests. People poking their heads in all day saying, "Got a minute? Got a minute?"

Slam the door on those poking heads. Those incessant talking heads give you a life in which you have not learned to say no. Once you learn it, teach it to your people, too. Make it an honorable thing. Your people's access to focused work will depend on their willingness to develop a little-used muscle that we call the No Muscle. If they never use this muscle, it won't perform for them when the chips are down. It will be too weak to work. Any request by any coworker or relative will pull them from your mission.

The key to teaching your people to develop the No Muscle is to first develop their Yes Muscle. If they will say yes to the things that are important to them, then saying no to what's not important will get easier and easier. Help them verbalize what they want. Make them say it out loud.

"Tina, you need to know what you want, know it in advance, and chances are you'll get it. It's easy to say no to something if you've already said yes to something better."

43. Think Friendly Customer Thoughts

There is only one boss: the customer.

—Sam Walton

Our customers are the origin, the originating source, of all the money we have and all the things we own. It's not the company that pays us, it's the customer. The company just passes the customer's money along to us. When we take a vacation, it's important to realize that *the customer has paid for it.* When we send a child to college, it's with our customer's money!

Sam Walton built his Wal-Mart empire knowing that there was always only one boss: the customer. "And the customer can fire everybody in the company," said Walton, "from the chairman on down, simply by spending his money somewhere else."

Why not begin motivating our people accordingly? Why not show our people the joy of treating that customer relationship as a real and genuine friendship? It could be, in the end, our ultimate competitive advantage.

Without our encouragement as leaders, the customer tends to fall off the radar screen. Without our asking the provocative and respectfully encouraging questions of our people, the customer can even become a "hassle" or a "necessary evil" in their lives.

In our zeal to bond with the people who report to us, we all too often commiserate and sympathize with their horror stories about how hard it is to please customers, how customers take advantage of them, why the phone ringing all day is such a problem for time-management...and we agree, and by agreeing, we unknowingly plant the seeds that allow customers to be treated coldly, stupidly, and in a very unfriendly way.

This defeats the whole purpose of our business! We're even willing to go further: It becomes the root cause of every business problem we have, indirectly. The whole purpose of your business is to take such good care of the customer that the customer makes it a habit of returning to your business and buying more and more every time. But this will only happen when your people consciously build relationships with your customers. When they actively, consciously, creatively, cleverly, strategically, artfully, and gently build the relationship instead of the company. Building the relationship does not come easy. It goes against our deepest habits, and it will never happen if your people see the customer as "a hassle...someone on the phone checking out prices...just an annoyance...someone interrupting me when I was just about to go on lunch...just a problem in my day...someone trying to return something... someone trying to challenge my years of expertise...some jerk...some idiot...."

The reason this kind of disrespect and even contempt for the customer sinks into the psyche of our people is a lack of ongoing encouragement to think any other way. In other words, a lack of leadership. In other words, you and me. A bad attitude toward the customer always comes, in some subtle way, from the top. We as leaders set the tone. We either ask the right questions that start the ball rolling in our employees' minds, or we do not. If I am a leader, I want to ask questions that respect my people's intelligence. I want to treat them as if they were master psychologists, as if they were experts in customer behavior and customer thinking patterns—because they are. I want to ask how we can build more trust with the customer. I want to ask how we can convert a seemingly simple phone call into a warm relationship that leads to the customer liking us and wanting to buy from us no matter what the price is. I want to ask how we can get the sales force to win the customer's trust and repeat business. I want to ask for advice and help with the psychology of the customer. I want to ask the questions that will motivate my own managers to start thinking in terms of lifetime customers instead of single transactions.

I might start a meeting with my team by saying, "Let's say you're a potential customer and you're calling my store. Let's say you're new in town and have no buying habits yet in this category of product. I'm the third store you have called. If I'm stressed and grumpy and I simply give you the price you wanted for a product you're curious about and hang up, I may have lost you forever. What does that matter? A loss of $69 won't kill us!

"But consider the lifetime impact—or even just the next 10 years. What if that customer spent even just $400 a year in this category but has, because of this bad original call with us, formed a buying habit with a competitor? (Most people go to certain stores because it feels comfortable to go there.) In 10 years, that customer would have spent $4,000. That's $4,000 lost in less than a minute on a bad phone call. If someone lost $4,000 in one minute from the cash register, would they still be working for us?"

Finally, in the end, I don't want to be too macho or too "professional" or too afraid of what people would think of me if I even used the word "friend" once in a while in my questions about how we can treat customers better. How would we treat that customer if that person were a dear friend?

Why is the word "friend" so rarely heard in the world of business relations? Are friends really better than customers? Does your best friend regularly come by and give you money to help with the mortgage payment? Does your friend pull out his checkbook after having a beer with you and say, "Here's a little something for your daughter's dental bill"?

Our customers do.

44. Best Time? Biggest Challenge

It's so hard when contemplated in advance, and so easy when you do it. —Robert Pirsig, philosopher and author

It's so important to use your best time for your biggest challenge. Of course you can't always do this. Sometimes challenges have a way of blowing out their own hole in your timetable. But whenever possible, see if you can *match up* your prime biological (emotional, physical, mental) time with the big job or big communications you have to do.

Many leaders are at their best in the first hours of the morning; others hit their prime in the late morning; others still, in the afternoon. Whichever is your best time to shine, don't waste it on trivial, low-return activities. Invest that energy and peak attention into the big challenge you've been procrastinating about.

Most of us confuse pleasure with happiness—we find great pleasure in spending our highest-energy state on small tasks, taking them out with relish and flair, blowing away all these minor little must-do's with great bursts of energy and good cheer. But all the while that big thing is lurking, waiting until we're tired and cranky to be fully contemplated...which is why it gets put off so often.

Know ahead of time what your biggest challenge is. Set it up to be *taken out with massive, unstoppable action* while you are at your most resourceful and energetic. That is the ultimate source of a leader's professional happiness...the feeling of accomplishment you get when you take out the big thing!

The look on your face alone will motivate others to follow you.

45. Use 10 Minutes Well

Man must not allow the clock and the calendar to blind him to the fact that each moment of his life is a miracle and a mystery. —H.G. Wells

Contemporary philosopher William Irwin was asked what he thought the secret of effective leadership was. His answer was, "Learn to use 10 minutes intelligently. It will pay you huge dividends."

Often what separates a great leader from a lousy manager is just that: the ability to use 10 minutes well.

The Irwin quote is one that we have on our office wall, reminding us that it really helps to have short, motivating quotations posted in plain view. It is a way to wake yourself up to your potential. Especially when you only have 10 minutes before your next appointment. Will you use it well? Or will you kill time?

Our recent visit to a very successful leader's office was enhanced by our noticing these words posted on the wall behind his desk—also a great guideline for using 10 minutes well:

The Most Important Words in the English Language:

5 most important words: *I am proud of you!*

4 most important words: *What is your opinion?*

3 most important words: *If you please.*

2 most important words: *Thank you.*

1 most important word: *You.*

And sometimes that powerful leadership item we have not *found* time to do can be *made* to fit into the next 10-minute window.

46. Know What You Want to Grow

> Discipline is the bridge between goals and
> accomplishments. —Jim Rohn, author
> and motivator

Most managers, especially those who struggle with "making a plan," place the plan's numbers down around sixth on their daily priority list. Most struggling managers place these things above the "plan" in their priority hierarchy:

1. Not upsetting other people's feelings.
2. The commitment to looking extremely busy.
3. Firefighting and problem-solving.
4. Explaining and justifying other people's performances, both up and down the ladder.
5. Being liked.

We saw a brilliant business consultant come into a struggling, financially failing company and turn everything around. He did it by altering priorities. The first thing he did was put huge scoreboards up all over the company conference and meeting room to reflect daily sales numbers and activity.

In the company's past, numbers had been an embarrassment. They were whispered about at the end of the month. If people weren't hitting good numbers, the management spent all its time listening to the reasons.

The salespeople had become good salespeople, but what they were learning to sell was their *excuses*, not their product. All management meetings focused on "circumstances, issues, and situations that prevent us from succeeding."

The other day, we spoke to an operations manager at a company that was falling far short of its business projections.

"We're not making plan," he said.

"Why not?"

"The economy. The weather. The war. The way kids are brought up today. The lack of good candidates for positions here. Company dysfunction. Industry decline. Government regulations. Competition moving in. No budget for sales training."

"Other than that, what's in your way?"

As we sat in on their company meetings, we observed that all the management meetings were about those subjects. All their meetings focused on the obstacles to success.

What you focus on grows. Focus on numbers, and they, too, will grow.

47. Soften Your Heart

> He is only advancing in life whose heart is getting
> softer, his blood warmer, his brain quicker, and his
> spirit entering into living peace.
> —John Ruskin, philosopher and author

People who really succeed in leadership and in sales transform the entire activity away from the concept of managing and selling (even though they have high respect for that) into the day-to-day concept of building relationships.

They always think in terms of their relationships with other people: How can I make it better? How can I serve them? How can I contribute to their life today? How can I show them a demonstration of my commitment to them? How can I make them happier? How can I make it easier for them to access this information? There is a continual expansion of the friendly side of the relationship. A leader knows that communication solves all problems. Avoidance worsens all problems.

No leadership agreement was ever made outside of a conversation. So have your conversations be vital. Have a lot of conversations today and make them warm and comfortable. Have them all lead you to your ultimate goal.

Master teacher Lance Secretan has written 13 books on leadership, and sums up his findings this way: "Leadership is not so much about technique and methods as it is about opening the heart. Leadership is about inspiration—of oneself and of others. Great leadership is about human experiences, not processes. Leadership is not a formula or a program, it is a human activity that comes from the heart and considers the hearts of others."

48. Coach Your People to Complete

Nothing is so fatiguing as the eternal hanging on of an uncompleted task. —William James

If your people become more and more burned out and fatigued, it's up to you to help them redirect a course of action that leads them to the completion of previous projects.

Once we went to hear Cheryl Richardson give a presentation to "Coach U" in Phoenix, and it was the first time we went to one of their meetings. We didn't know her or anything about Coach U. But we settled in for the talk.

Richardson stood up and said to all of us, "Can you come up with a list of the top 10 things that are incomplete, that need to get done in your life? Can you come up with that list?"

Of course, everyone could. So we did. And then she told us an example of how she coaches her clients. She said she had a massage therapist who came in to see her, and she said to him, "What's the issue?"

The client said, "I need more business."

She said, "Okay, I want you to write down the top 10 things that you need to complete in your life." And the client wrote them down.

Then she said, "Now, I want you to make a commitment that you will get those complete."

The massage therapist said, "Okay, but that's not why I'm here to see you. I'm here because I need more business."

Cheryl Richardson said, "I know that. Get this done, and you'll get more business."

Her coaching client said, "What? This doesn't have any-thing to do with getting more business."

Cheryl explained, "Actually, everything that is incomplete in your life is what I call an *energy drain*. And that is stopping you from having more business."

"Well, that doesn't make any sense to me."

Cheryl said, "I only do this for a *living*! I counsel lots of clients who all have this same thing. Are you willing to try it? If not, let's forget this relationship."

"Well, okay, I guess, yeah. I need to get those things done anyway." So he made a commitment to get three of the 10 done by the next meeting.

So, the following week, he reported in and said, "I com-pleted my assignment."

And Cheryl asked, "What happened?"

"Amazing! Even before the first week was over, three new people have called me out of the blue, and filled up my calen-dar."

And Cheryl says, "That's how it works."

We never forgot that lesson, and have retaught it ever since. It's not just that your people have all those incompletes out there, but the underlying thought of it, the subconscious knowledge *is the energy drain*.

It's draining their productivity and vitality away. Help them clean those incompletes up and their motivation will surprise you.

49. Do the Math on Your Approach

We make a living by what we get, but we make a life by what we give. —Winston Churchill

You will really enjoy motivating others if you start thinking of your life as a mathematical equation. We first saw the fun and benefit of this when our good friend and company CEO Duane Black solved the equation on two flipcharts in front of a grateful gathering of managers.

Here it is: When you are positive (picturing the math sign: +) you *add* something to any conversation or meeting you are part of. That's what being positive does, it adds.

When you are negative (–), you *subtract* something from the conversation, the meeting, or the relationship you are part of. If you are negative enough times, you subtract so much from the relationship that there is no more relationship left. It's simple math. It's the law of the universe up there on the flip chart of life: positive adds, negative subtracts.

As in math, when you add a negative, it diminishes the total. Add a negative person to the team, and the morale and spirit (and, therefore, productivity and profit) of the team is diminished.

When you are a positive leader with positive thoughts about the future and the people you lead, you *add* something to every person you talk to. You bring something of value to every communication. Even every e-mail and voice mail that's positive adds something to the life of the person who receives it. Because positive (+) always adds something.

It runs even deeper than that. If you think positive thoughts throughout the day, you are adding to your own deep inner experience of living. You are bringing a plus to your own spirit and energy with each positive thought. Your negative thoughts take away from the experience of being alive. They rob you of your energy.

Say this to yourself: *I like this math. I like its simplicity. I can now do this math throughout my day. When I am experiencing negative thoughts about my team or my to-do list, I know it's time to take a break and regroup and refresh. It's time to call a time-out, close my eyes, and relax into my purpose and my mission. It's time to slow down and breathe into it. I take a lot of quick breaks like that during the day, and this practice is changing my life for the better. It is making me stronger and more energetic than ever before.*

Your own strength and energy motivates others. Or, as Carlos Castaneda said, "We either make ourselves miserable, or we make ourselves strong. The amount of work is the same."

50. Count Yourself in

> To decide to be at the level of choice, is to take responsibility for your life and to be in control of your life. —Arbie M. Dale, psychologist and author

Leaders who take ownership motivate more effectively than leaders who pass themselves off as victims of the corporate structure or upper management. That's because they have made a conscious decision to *live at the level of choice.* Throughout their day, their people hear them talk of "buying in." They are always heard saying, "Count me in. I'm in on that."

The reason leaders living at the level of choice say, "Count me in," is not because they're apple-polishing, bootlicking company people. As a matter of fact, they don't much care who their company is! They're going to play full out for the company because it makes life more interesting, it makes work a better experience, and it's more fun. Whether it's a volleyball game at a picnic or the company's latest big project, *it is more fun* to buy in and play hard.

Let's say the company orders everyone to break up into experimental teams. The manager with the victim's mind may say, "I'll wait and see. What's this new stuff they are throwing at us now? It's not enough that I have to work for a living; I've got to play all these games. What's this woo-woo, touchy-feely team stuff? I'm not going to buy into it yet; I'll wait and see. I'll give it five years."

Meanwhile the owner-leader is saying, "Hey, I'm not going to judge this thing. That's a waste of mental energy. I'm buying in. Why? Because it deserves to be bought into? No. I don't care if it deserves to be bought into or not. I am buying in because it gives me more energy, it makes working more fun, I deserve to be happy at work, and I know from experience that buying into things works."

True leadership inspires a spirit of buy-in. It's a spirit that has no relationship to whether the company deserves being bought into. The source of the buy-in is a personal commitment to have a great experience of life. True leaders don't negatively personalize their companies.

You stand for mental health. And when other people see that spirit in you, they are motivated to live that way, too, by positive example. They can see that it works. In sports, it's sometimes easier to see the value of this spirit. It seems obviously reasonable for an athlete to say, "I don't care if I'm playing for a minor league team or a major league team, it's in my self-interest to play full out when I play." In companies, though, that would be a rare position to take. Self-motivated leaders are rare.

True leaders don't wait for the company to catch up to their lead. They *take* the lead. They don't wait for the company to give them something good to follow. No company will ever catch up with a great individual. A great individual will always be more creative than the company as a whole.

Martin Luther King said, "If a man is called to be a street sweeper, he should sweep streets as Michelangelo painted or Beethoven composed music or Shakespeare wrote poetry."

51. First, Just Relax

> A frightened captain makes a frightened crew.
> —Lister Sinclair, playwright and broadcaster

The great music teacher and motivator of artists Rodney Mercado had a simple recipe for success. He said, "There are only two principles that you need to get to play great music or to live a great life: concentration and relaxation. And that's it. That is it."

⌘⌘⌘

Scott Richardson recalls this remark and what he said back to Mercado: "What? That doesn't have anything to do with music!"

"It has everything to do with music."

And the way he taught relaxation was: "You need to have the maximum relaxation. For instance, if you want to play faster, Scott, you need to relax more. If you want to play louder, you need to relax more. If you want more sound coming out, you need to relax more."

Up to this point in my life, it sounded like someone saying, "Well, if you want to become a cowboy, go to Harvard." It didn't make any sense. It seemed like a contradiction.

Doesn't it sound like a contradiction? If you're going to motivate people, don't you want to get them all hyped up and worked up? That's what I had always thought: Light a fire! Get the lead out of your pants!

So up to this point in my life, if I wanted to play faster, I would get hyped and tense up. And I would try harder. In any aspect of my life where I was trying to get more of something, I would become more tense from trying.

But Mercado said, "I'm going to play a passage of music and I want you to just listen for a moment."

I did. I don't remember the passage played at the time, but he almost ripped the strings off the violin. It was a virtuoso passage, but it sounded like he was going to make the strings just fly apart, there was so much sound and motion being produced. And I was awed.

"Now, Scott, I want you to put your arm on top of my forearm while I play this passage, and feel what's going on while I'm doing this."

When I put my arm on top of his forearm and he played this passage (and by the way, I'm trying to hang on for dear life, because his arm was flying), I was stunned, because his arm was almost totally relaxed. There was no tension in the muscles!

And all of a sudden, I got it.

Getting it changed my entire concept of playing the violin, but it also changed my concept of *what I was doing in life*. I had been tensing and straining for success instead of relaxing for it.

The same formula works for a sprinter in track and field. What most sprinters do when they try to run faster is to put more effort into it. And they don't realize it but they tense up their muscles and their times actually drop. Trying harder slows them down! The sprinters don't realize that they're at their peak state of relaxation during their fastest times.

I saw this firsthand while on the Brigham Young University track team when I was in a physical education class. I thought I was pretty tough stuff, so I raced one guy who wasn't on the track team. The guy barely beat me, but he was straining and out of control, and he just stumbled over the finish line. Then I met another guy who was one of the top sprinters on the BYU track team, and I challenged him to a race. We took off and he beat me by a wide margin. Because there he was, Mr. Mercado's theory in motion: totally relaxed, totally fluid, and he just flew by me.

So that principle is something that I have now adopted anytime I'm doing anything. If I'm in front of a jury, or my company, or any other group while I'm speaking, I know that the secret is relaxation, as counterintuitive as that may seem. Because what do most people do? They get nervous, they get tense, and their performance drops. But because of the training Mercado gave me, anytime I feel any tension at all, I slow down and relax all the more. His words always come back to me: "If you start shaking, there's only one way you can shake. You have to be tense. If you relax, you cannot shake. If you start shaking, that's a sign that you're not relaxing."

⌘⌘⌘

We have attended countless conventions and retreats where the CEO totally blows an opportunity to motivate his people by stepping up to the podium and reading nervously from a script, or making a brief and tense talk that leaves everyone flat. A vice president of a large bank said to us of his CEO, after the CEO had addressed 200 senior managers at a yearly conference:

"Did you hear him? Did you see him? I mean, we wait all year to hear his words to us and he gives this nervous, brief, memorized talk! Like he couldn't be bothered to really talk to us!"

"He was obviously nervous about his talk."

"That's my point! To him, it was something he had to do. He obviously didn't want to do it. So his whole focus was on himself and what little he could get away with doing."

"What do you want? He's not a public speaker."

"Well, if he's going to lead a large company and ask us to hit the goals he's asking us to, he darn well better learn to be a public speaker! Because it's not about him, it's about us. We deserve better. We deserve someone talking to us, and I mean really talking to us. From the heart. Loud and strong and with passion and without notes."

"So, how do you *really* feel about his talk?"

"That he came across as a pathetic little ball of ego who doesn't deserve to lead this company because he refuses to put himself on the line. We would have been more motivated if he had called in sick."

If you're in a situation where you have to give a talk to your people and you feel tense, like it's not coming from the heart, practice relaxing on the spot. If your legs start to shake, don't worry. It's just feedback time, and the feedback from your body is that you're not relaxed. If you're relaxed, you cannot shake; it's physically impossible. Once you relax, you become a much better speaker. So don't just practice the talk you're going to give. Practice relaxing, too.

52. Don't Throw the Quit Switch

Most people succeed because they are determined
to. People of mediocre ability sometimes achieve
outstanding success because they don't know when
to quit. —George Allen, football coach

Every human being has a certain, little-known brain part in common: a Quit Switch. Some people, out of lifelong habit, throw the Quit Switch at the first sign of frustration. Their workout gets difficult, so they throw the switch and go home. Their day of phone calls gets frustrating, so they throw the switch and go for coffee with a coworker for two hours of sympathetic negativity.

Everyone has a Quit Switch. Not everyone knows it.

Get to know it. Notice yourself flipping the switch. You can't quit and you won't quit until you throw the switch. A human being is built, like any animal, to persist until a goal is reached. Watch children get what they want and you'll see the natural, built-in persistence.

Somewhere along the way, though, we learn about this little switch. Soon, we start flipping the switch. Some of us begin by flipping it after a severe frustration, and then start flipping it after medium frustration, and until finally it's thrown in the face of any discomfort at all. We quit.

If you weren't in the habit of throwing the switch too early, you would achieve virtually any goal you ever set. You would never give up on your team. You'd make every month's sales goal. You'd even lose all the weight you ever wanted to lose. You would achieve anything you wanted because you would not throw the switch.

The Quit Switch is something you can focus on, learn about, and make work *for* you instead of against you. Whether you flip it early or late is only habit. The switch-flipping habit is misinterpreted as a lack of willpower, courage, drive, or desire, but that's nonsense. It's a habit. And like any habit, it can be replaced with another habit.

Make it your habit *not* to throw the Quit Switch early in any process. Do not quit on yourself as a leader or on your team as producers. The less of a quitter you are, the more of a motivator you become.

53. Lead With Enthusiasm

Nothing great was ever created without enthusiasm.
—Ralph Waldo Emerson

All the world's a stage. You are a great actor on that stage. When it is your turn to appear in a scene, be enthusiastic, especially if you have something to fire your team up about. If you have something to convince them of, try being really enthusiastic about what you have to say, simply as a place to come from. When your employees speak in return, be enthusiastic. Glow. Sparkle. Radiate leadership and solutions. Pump yourself up. Take it to an even higher level.

When you're ready to get the team involved, don't fade out... remember you are *acting* enthusiastic. You are an actor, and a good one. Finish strong. Enthusiasm is contagious. People love to be around it. It makes them smile and shake their heads... it can even make them laugh with pleasure at the dynamo that is you.

Most managers make the mistake of not doing this. They act reserved and cool and "professional." They don't act "professional" because they *are* professional; they do it because they're scared (about how they're coming across), and they think if they act cool they will be safe.

We spoke with Jeremy about a talk we had him give to his team. "You seemed a little less than enthusiastic about this new commission system, Jeremy."

"Really? I didn't realize that."

"That's the point."

"What do you mean?" Jeremy said.

"You aren't realizing your lack of enthusiasm in front of your team because you are choosing not to be conscious of it."

"How is it a choice?"

"You are choosing to be less than enthusiastic."

"Oh, I don't think so. It doesn't feel like I'm making any kind of choice." Jeremy said.

"You speak Spanish, don't you, Jeremy?"

"Yes, I do. I'm bilingual. It helps with certain customers."

"Did you realize that you gave your talk to your team in English? Were you aware of that?"

"Yes, of course."

"Did you choose that?"

"Of course I chose it! The whole team speaks English. What are you driving at here?" Jeremy asked.

"Your choice to speak in English was as clear and definite a choice as your choice to be unenthusiastic. You have an equally clear choice about enthusiasm (or no enthusiasm) as you do about choosing between English and Spanish. We recommend you stop choosing to be unenthusiastic with your people."

Jeremy said nothing.

"Cool doesn't sell. A chilly professionalism doesn't make much of an impression. It is immediately forgotten, along with the idea you are promoting."

Enthusiasm comes from the Greek words *en theos*, which translate to "the God within," the most spirited and spiritual you. You times 10; the you when you were a little kid riding your bike with no hands.

Enthusiasm is contagious. If you are excited about your idea, everyone else will be excited. That's how it works. Always remember Emerson's observation, "Nothing great was ever created without enthusiasm."

You can lead with enthusiasm, or you can lead without enthusiasm. Those are your choices. One choice leads to a highly motivated team; the other leads to long-term problems.

"But how can I be enthusiastic when I'm not?" Jeremy finally said.

We hear managers ask that question that all the time. The answer is easy. The way to *be* enthusiastic is to *act* enthusiastic. There isn't a person in the world who can tell the difference if you put your heart and soul into your acting. And about a minute and a half into your acting, the funniest thing starts to happen: the enthusiasm becomes real. You do feel it. And so does your team.

54. Encourage Concentration

The first law of success is concentration, to bend all
the energies to one point, and to go directly to that
point, looking neither to the right, nor to the left.
—William Mathews, journalist

The other principle that Professor Mercado believed in was concentration, or focus. And to drive it home to his students, he had a bizarre system. Scott recalls: Professor Mercado had us play music recitals, as most teachers do. But at these recitals, he would have us play our pieces twice. The first time we would play them as we would at any standard recital. We would play "Mary Had a Little Lamb" on the violin and the audience would politely clap. And then, after that performance was done and everybody had a chance to play the traditional way, Mercado would say, "Okay, now we're going to play it again. Everyone's going to have a chance to perform their piece again."

But this time, as the performers were performing, Mercado would pass out slips of paper to the audience. The slips would have instructions written on them, such as, *Go up to the performer and tickle his ear. Sing "Yankee Doodle Dandy."* Mercado would even say to the performer's accompanist, "Speed up." "Slow down." "Stop."

Mercado would then physically come up to us while we were playing and he would do things even more radical than that! He would take our bow away. He would untune our strings so you couldn't get any sound out of the string. Then, he would start tuning the instrument back up. Basically, all hell would break loose during these second performances.

And when it was over, he would ask each one of us, "Which performance was better? The first one, or the second one, where all hell was breaking loose?"

I normally ask people what they think the answer is, and some people say the first way. But invariably, the second performance was better, the one in which we were most distracted! And we all admitted that. And then he would ask us why.

The answer was pretty obvious to those who had lived through it, and that was because we were "forced" to totally concentrate and focus on our music internally. We had been compelled to exclude every other environmental impact or influence and just wipe it out. If we had paid any attention to what was going on around us, we would have become hopelessly lost. By totally focusing internally on what we were attempting to produce—the music—and excluding everything else, including our accompanist, we performed fantastically in the face of extraordinary odds. You can't imagine anything that difficult.

The lesson was huge. And I use the lesson this way: the next time I'm upset by the chaos swirling all around me, I *use it* to focus myself even more.

⌘⌘⌘

If you want your people to be truly inspired by your example, show them how to use distractions to focus them even more, not less. Show them how it's done.

55. Inspire Inner Stability

Becoming a leader is synonymous with becoming yourself. It is precisely that simple, and it is also that difficult. —Warren Bennis

People look so hard for stability. All the leaders we coach and work with on some level or another are secretly trying to find more stability in their work, in their careers, and especially in their companies.

But the key to stability is not to look *outside yourself* for it. It's useless to try to find it from your company or from your industry. It only works to look back inside. You need to turn the mirror around so you can see yourself. You need to find it inside your own enthusiasm for work. And sometimes that inner enthusiasm must be built from scratch, from improvisation.

Psychologist Nathaniel Branden puts it this way:

Chances are, when you were young, you were told, in effect, "Listen, kid, here is the news: Life is not about you. Life is not about what you want. What you want is not important. Life is about doing what others expect of you." If you accepted this idea, later on you wondered what had happened to your fire. Where had your enthusiasm for living gone?

Ask yourself the following questions: *Do I feel good about myself at the end of the day? Am I proud of my leadership today? Do I feel that wonderful little feeling that I get when we've had a good day and we feel like we've really nailed it?* If so, that opinion is vital (and visible) to the people I want to motivate.

If you can consciously build that level of confidence in yourself as a leader, then you can put stability into your career. That's where real stability comes from, especially in this era of rapid-fire external changes.

The marketplace changes, each industry changes, the whole world changes. Every morning as we open up the newspaper or turn on the news, something radical is different. Something important will never be the same. This rapid change is terrifying to unstable people. Unstable people wish things would just stay the same.

Does anything motivate people more than to be in the presence of a leader with inner stability and self-esteem? We build self-esteem in small increments, just like athletes build strength. They don't do it overnight. They do it day-by-day, adding a little more weight to the bar, adding a little more distance to the run. Pretty soon, they are magnificent, powerful, wonderful athletes. The same is true with leadership; it happens the same way. A little bit every day, a little better at communication, a little better at delegation, a little better at servant leadership, a little bit better at listening to people. Getting 2 percent, maybe 4 percent, better. No more than that. It's conscious and it is inspiring to be around.

56. Give Up Being Right

I must follow the people. Am I not their leader?

—Benjamin Disraeli

One of the things that happens with a lot of people we've worked with over the years is that when they get promoted to a management position, they feel that it's very important that everybody sees that *they know what they're doing.* They twist that into a drive to be right. They think people will only admire them if they're right about things, and by doing this, they make it really hard for themselves to be human with their people. They make it hard for themselves to admit that they're wrong and to say to other people, "You know what? You're right about that."

A really strong, motivational leader who is admired and respected is one who does not *have to* be right about anything. Ever. It is much more powerful to say to someone, "You know, now that I've listened to you, one thing I've realized is that you are right about that. And I'm going to take some steps to get that done." That's a person who will eventually motivate others.

Being right is never going to matter in the long run. What's going to matter in the long run is achieving something. I can be wrong about absolutely everything day in, day out, and still be a wonderfully great leader. Why? Because I brought out the best in my people. I've taught them to make their own decisions. I have drawn out their strengths, their loyalties, their high performance, and all the numbers have tumbled in my direction.

57. Wake Yourself Up

> Too many people are thinking of security instead of opportunity. They seem to be more afraid of life than death. —James F. Bymes, former Secretary of State

Change will scare my people to the degree that it scares me.

Another way to consciously build my inner strength as a leader is to increase my awareness of what life is like, what the world is like, and what the business community is like. As I become more aware of that, I become a better leader. I don't want to just put my head into the sand and say, "But we've been doing it this way for 20 years." I don't want to always be heard saying, "I don't want to think about it, I don't want to be aware that anything's changed. I just want everything to be like it used to be, I want people to be the way they used to be." But if I don't want to have a real understanding of what people are like today, especially younger people and how they're perceiving life, my leadership skills will decline over the years, and pretty soon I'll become irrelevant.

As Nathaniel Branden writes in *Self-Esteem at Work*

We now live in a global economy characterized by rapid change, accelerating scientific and technological breakthroughs, and an unprecedented level of competitiveness. These developments create demands for higher levels of education and training than were required from previous generations. Everyone acquainted with business culture knows this. What is not understood is that these developments also create new demands on our psychological resources. Specifically, these developments ask for greater capacity for innovation…self management…personal responsibility… and self direction.

It used to be that leaders were led by other leaders, managers were managed by other managers, and there wasn't much wiggle room in between. We were told what to do, then we told other people what to do, and it was basically a hierarchical, military-type system. But now things are so complex and ever-changing—it's like calling audible plays at the line of scrimmage every single time, instead of running regular plays.

Life has changed profoundly. And it will continue to change even faster as time goes on. That's good news for a leader committed to being more and more awake to it.

58. Always Show Them

I hear and I forget. I see and I remember. I do and I understand. —Confucius

A lot of great sports players are promoted to coach, but it just doesn't quite work. Sometimes, it turns out, they're just not very good at it. And there's a reason. It's not mysterious. They are simply not totally *conscious* of what it was that made them great players. A lot of what they did as players was intuitive and subconscious. It was the feel of the thing. And so they have a very hard time teaching it to others and communicating it *because they didn't even know what it was.*

The best batting coach of all time was Charlie Lau. He taught a baseball player by the name of George Brett how to hit. And as you may know, George Brett was one of the greatest hitters of all time. George Brett was a magnificent hitter, hitting in the high .300s all the time. But Charlie Lau—his coach, his instructor, his teacher—had a lifetime batting average of .255! Charlie Lau was a mediocre hitter at best. But because Lau had to struggle so hard just to stay in the majors, just to keep his job, he learned hitting inside out. He became extremely conscious of how it was done. Therefore, he was great at teaching it.

When you figure something out, anything, that your people are not doing up to the level that you'd like them to be doing it, *show* them what to do. Take the bat in your own hands and show them how to hit.

Christina wanted our opinion on a problem she was having with her team.

"My people aren't great with customers," Christina said. "I believe they leave a lot of business on the table."

"Tell us how you'd like your people to be different."

"Well, here's what I think," said Christina. "I bet if my people talked to customers a little differently, asked them more questions, got more interested in their lives, that they'd find out a few other areas in which they could help them out. They'd find out areas where we might have a product or a service that would help the customer. Instead, my people just sell people things, they're just order-takers, and our sales aren't as high as they could be if they took a greater interest in the customer."

"What have you done about that?"

"First, I sent that opinion around in an e-mail, and that didn't go over very well," said Christina.

"Of course it wouldn't."

"Right," she said. "Then I called some of them and said, 'I want you to get your people to do more of this!'"

"Did that go well?"

"No."

"What else did you do?"

"I called HR," said Christina. "I told HR we really needed training in this. Relationships. The upsell."

"How did the training go?"

"Still waiting," said Christina. "I'm still waiting for an answer to my request for it."

"Christina, do this yourself! A true leader, a really powerful leader, who's consciously motivating others to great performance, will *show them how to do it*. A true leader will figure out what it is that she wants her people to do and then will go in and demonstrate it."

We sat in later as Christina talked to her team.

"Here, let me work with you today," she told them. "I want to talk to customers who come in. All I'd like you to do is assist me, be there, help out, ask questions if you can think of them. But let's you and I—*you and I*—talk to some customers as they come in."

Christina learned to *show* people the way she wished they would do it. She realized that the best way to communicate this was to do it herself. That was her new leverage point, and that was the way her people got excited and understood quickly.

If you just tell your people, "I want you to do more of that, you've got to get better at that," it falls on deaf ears, and sometimes even worse. Sometimes it causes people to *defend* how they're not doing it. It causes people to tell you, "I don't have time to do that." To really motivate, talk less and demonstrate more.

59. Focus Like a Camera

Most of the successful people I've known are the ones who do more listening than talking.
—Bernard Baruch

We want to introduce a kind of leadership that we find in only one out of every 10 leaders we work with. We call it *focused leadership*. It's the ability on the part of a leader to be absolutely focused. And what we mean by focused is not hard-core, intense concentration, like you're forcing something. It's really the opposite. It's a much more relaxed sense of focus. Imagine focusing a camera: You're looking through the camera and it looks fuzzy, and as you turn the focus dial or knob, you don't have to jam it or whack it or slam it. All you have to do is move it very gently one way or another, and all of a sudden, the whole picture comes into focus. That same thing can happen with your *outlook* as a leader.

Someone will walk into your office, sit down, and notice that you are beginning to focus on her like a camera, because there's that internal dial in you that is very slowly moving until the person across the way comes into a gentle, relaxed, absolute focus. And now, you may breathe a sigh, and take a deep breath, and say, "Tell me what's on your mind. How're you doing? Let's talk about this issue here."

Your employee will pick up on this gentle, relaxed sense of focus, and be honored by it. She will be thinking: *It's as if we're the only two people in the world right now. It feels like we're on a desert island and we've got all the time in the world.*

You will be thinking, *And I'm listening to you, and you and I are going to get to the bottom of this. But not in a rushed way, and not because we have to. But because that's where the conversation will take us in an open way. In a way that honors you and acknowledges you, and hears you, and we just talk. We're going to exchange some ideas, I'm going to ask you some questions, and we're going to find out what the two of us think about this. I'm not going to tell you what to do. And I'm not someone who's got an agenda that's hidden that I'm going to reveal to you bit by bit as I talk to you. I'm wide open. I'm like a camera.*

And you are a great leader.

You already know the other kind of leader, the not-so-great one: the leader who comes into meetings carrying his electronic organizer, and while he's sitting in the meeting, he'll be returning e-mails, picking up his vibrating cell phone every two or three minutes to see who it is, and also trying to be present in the meeting. He's thinking he's multitasking, but really, he's just not focused. And everyone who runs into that leader feels diminished by the exchange.

We talked to Richie about a leader of his who behaves that way.

"I always feel about him that he's someone who has no time for me," Richie said. "That's someone who'd really rather not be talking to me right now."

That "leader" knows that, on some level, all of the 100 people he communicated with that week in some form—some by e-mail, some by text, some by fax, some by phone, some in person, some in the hallway—all 100 people have been dishonored by this behavior.

Deep down, the dysfunctional manager knows it. And so he has an uneasy feeling. He must fix this sense of things not going right. But rather than slowing down, he speeds up!

Once we told a manager who behaved this way that he ought to wear a sign around his neck.

"What do you mean a sign around my neck?"

"You ought to wear a sign, like people do in treatment centers when they're trying to solve a personal issue, and the sign should read, 'I HAVE NO TIME FOR YOU.'"

He said nothing.

"You also might want to have your e-mail send an automatic reply to people that reads, 'I HAVE NO TIME FOR YOU.'"

"Why would I do that? I could never do that," he said.

"You're doing it now. You're sending that message now. This way, you'd just be more up front about it."

When we coach people to open up and focus on their people, like a camera, it actually saves them time in the long run. Because it takes a lot less time to manage a motivated, trusting team than it does to work with a demoralized, upset team.

60. Think of Managing as Easy

Always think of what you have to do as easy and it will be. —Emile Coue, psychologist

A thought is more than a thought, it creates your reality. The role of thought in managing people and results cannot be overestimated. What you *think* about how hard your work is more important than any so-called interpreted "reality" about your work.

If you think motivating people is hard, it is hard. There's no difference. As Shakespeare said, "There is nothing bad nor good, but thinking makes it so."

If you think it's hard and uncomfortable to get on the telephone, then it is. If you think you're happy and relaxed picking up the phone, then you are.

It's important to see the power that thought has in the world of leadership. If you're thinking thoughts that bring you down, you're not going to have a very good "people day." Leadership requires high levels of humanity. To be a great at leader, we need to share our humanity and receive our people's humanity all day.

You can be a leader who is successful at motivating others. Thought is the key.

When Napoleon Hill wrote *Think and Grow Rich* his point was that you can think yourself into a perfect position to become successful. Many people have followed his instructions and done it—many who were not as smart as we are. We can also do it. Is it easy? Actually it can be. For as the great and celebrated philosopher Coue said, "Always think of what you have to do as easy and it will be."

One thing's for sure: It's never any harder than you think it is.

61. Cultivate the Power of Reassurance

In organizations, real power and energy is generated through relationships. The patterns of relationships and the capacities to form them are more important than tasks, functions, roles, and positions.
—Margaret Wheatly, management consultant

One of the most valuable additions to a person's life that a leader can provide is reassurance. You won't hear about it in any management seminars, and that's a shame, because there's nothing more motivating than a healthy dose of reassurance. How many leadership books focus on it? None. How important is it as a management tool? It's the *most* important tool.

How many times during the day do you ask yourself, *How reassuring was I in that conversation?* How many times before a conversation do you ask yourself, *Now, how can I be really reassuring to this person, so that he leaves reassured that everything's going to be all right, and that he's got the skills to do this job?*

If you integrate *reassurance* into your personal system and managerial approach, things will change on your team. The state of mind of your people will be altered for the better.

People look to their leaders for reassurance. Period. Truth is, they don't get that reassurance most of the time. They get the opposite. They get the impression that the team is racing and behind the gun. Their manager's demeanor and language cries out, "We've got to go, go, go. I'm late, I'm sorry I'm late for my meeting with you." "I'm on the phone and it's rush, rush, and we're behind the eight-ball, and it's crazy around here."

The problem with that message is that you are not reassured. When a you do the chaos act and convey a crisis mentality, it's not reassuring. The concept that counters all of that and cures it forever is the concept of reassurance.

62. Phase Out Disagreement

The best way to have a good idea is to have lots of ideas. —Linus Pauling, Nobel Prize scientist

When you listen to another person during a meeting or in a one-on-one, one of the best things you can do is to stop disagreeing. In other words, listen for the value in what someone has to say; don't listen for whether you agree with her, because every time you disagree with your employees, you throw them off balance and put them in a worse mood than they were before.

If I constantly disagree with you, what will you do? You will begin to defend yourself, won't you? All humans do. You go on the defensive. You don't just say, "Oh, okay, yeah, I see your point of view. Yes sir, you're right, and I was wrong, and so that's good. I'm in a better mood, now. What else do you disagree with?" That won't happen.

If you're going to disagree with someone, accept the consequences. The main consequence is you've lowered that person's mood. And the consequence of putting someone in a bad mood? That person's not going to do a very good job. People do not do well when they're in a bad mood. Their energy goes away. However, if you were to start listening for the value in what people had to say, instead of whether you disagreed with them, their moods would still be good as you talked. In fact, by listening for the value in everyone in a team meeting instead of listening for whether you agree, the mood of the whole room will rise. You can influence an entire team meeting by having it be your personal policy as a leader to always listen for the value in what someone has to say.

Most managers don't do that. Most managers let someone talk, and then say, "No, that's not right. I don't agree with that."

Then they wonder why their employee now feels undervalued. But it was the manager's obsession with disagreement that made the employee feel undervalued.

How does making someone feel stupid make him ready to be more motivated? Does anyone ever think, "Okay, you've made me feel stupid, I'm really ready to work hard now. I'm feelin' stupid, let's go!"

Most managers tell us, "Well, if I disagree, I disagree. All I'm doing is disagreeing." Okay, but every time you disagree, you're going to challenge somebody and make him feel stupid, and that's the consequence. Sometimes you *have* to disagree. But the less you do that, the better the team will be for you. The more motivated your people will be.

63. Keep Learning

> Leaders grow; they are not made.
> —Peter Drucker

Stay on your learning curve. And let your people see you learning. Don't show them a "know-it-all" attitude all the time. Let them know that you are a work in progress. That will make it easier for them to approach you with good ideas.

Most managers are so insecure in their role that they continuously try to look like they know it all. They never go to seminars. They scorn the latest book on management theory. But this attitude is actually demoralizing to their followers. We all can learn something new about our profession every day. Little by little, we can add to our knowledge base, and that increases our professional strength and capacity to help others.

Happiness is growth. We are happy when we are growing. And happy people are more motivated than unhappy people.

64. Learn What Leadership Is Not

The great leaders are like the best conductors—they reach beyond the notes to reach the magic in the players. —Blaine Lee, management consultant

Managers make a big mistake when they get bossy. It is a sure sign of insecurity when you push the point that you're the boss. You can be decisive and courageous, and hold people accountable without ever being pushy and bossy about it.

Dee Hock, founder and CEO Emeritus of VISA International, put it this way

Control is not leadership; management is not leadership; leadership is leadership is leadership. If you seek to lead, invest at least 50 percent of your time leading yourself—your own purpose, ethics, principles, motivation, conduct. Invest at least 20 percent leading those with authority over you and 15 percent leading your peers. If you don't understand that you work for your mislabeled "subordinates," then you know nothing of leadership. You know only tyranny.

Those are strong words for the bossy. But the bossy are clueless about human nature, especially in these times. All of our people are thinkers. They aren't robots. The old style of militaristic leadership is no longer appropriate. It's no longer leadership.

Today's leaders find the magic in their players.

65. Hear Your People Out

I have more fun, and enjoy more financial success, when I stop trying to get what I want and start helping other people get what they want.
—Spencer Johnson, business author

How would we know what kind of a leader you are? There is one very fast way: We would ask the people who follow you. They know. And what they say is true. You are who *they say* you are. Listen to them! Understand them. People are highly motivated by listeners, listeners like you who "get" what their problems are. Always be mindful.

In the words of Thich Nhat Hanh:

When we are mindful, we notice that another person suffers. If one person suffers, that person needs to talk to someone in order to get relief. We have to offer our presence, and we have to listen deeply to the other person who is suffering. That is the practice of love—deep listening. But if we are full of anger, irritation, and prejudices, we don't have the capacity to listen deeply to the people we love. If people we love cannot communicate with us, then they will suffer more. Learning how to listen deeply is our responsibility. We are motivated by the desire to relieve suffering. That is why we listen. We need to listen with all our heart, without intention to judge, condemn, or criticize. And if we listen in that way for one hour, we are practicing true love. We don't have to say anything; we just need to listen.

To help your people get what they want, be mindful of them and listen to them until you find out what they really want. Then, make their goals fit inside the team objectives. Show them the link. That's how long-lasting motivation finally happens.

66. Play It Lightly

The leadership instinct you are born with is the back-bone. Then you develop the funny bone and the wish-bone that go with it. —Elaine Agather, former CEO, JPMorgan Chase Bank

The most motivated people we work with are not taking themselves all that seriously. The ones who struggle the most view the company's next success as their own mortgage payment or what holds their marriage together. The managers who are the most creative, productive, and innovative see business as a chess game, played for fun and challenge. They conceive of all kinds of lovely moves and counter strategies. And when they "lose," they just set up the pieces again even more excitedly.

The worst failures and most miserable people at work are the ones who take everything too seriously. They are grim, discouraged, and bitter. They use only 10 percent of their brains all day. Their brains, once so huge in childhood, are now hardened and contracted into resentment and worry.

Here's what the overly serious people miss: the fun, the creativity, the lighthearted ideas, the intuition, the good spirits, the easy energy, and the quick laughter that brings people close to each other. They miss that. So no wonder they fail at what they're doing. Anytime we take something that seriously, we will find ways to subtly and subconsciously run away from it all day. Secretly, we are like children. We resist the serious.

One of America's most respected scholars on organizational leadership is Warren Bennis. In his book *On Becoming a Leader* (Perseus Publishing, Revised Ed., 2003), he stresses the difference between a leader and a manager: "The leader innovates; the manager administrates. The leader focuses on people; the manager focuses on systems and structure. The leader inspires; the manager controls. The leader is his own person; the manager is a good soldier. The leader sees the long-term; the manager sees the short-term."

G.K. Chesterton once said that angels can fly only because they take themselves lightly. We say the same of leaders.

67. Keep All Your Smallest Promises

Great things are not done by impulse, but by a series of small things brought together.
—Vincent van Gogh

People are motivated by people they trust.

The trust of your people is not difficult to obtain. You can win it. And because it's so important for motivating them, you must win it. So you must never, ever be late to your own meetings. Ever. Such a thing will destroy all trust you've built up with seven out of 10 people, because it means to them that you cannot be counted on to keep your word.

We explained this to Jeff after working with his team for a while and noticing that he was not keeping any of his small promises.

"Hey, it's no biggie!" Jeff would say. "I'm a little late, or I forget to get somebody a parking pass, so what? I'm a big-picture guy. I'm not all that anal."

"It's your word, Jeff. If you can't keep it together in the small things, no one will trust it in any of the big things."

"Well," said Jeff, "What should I do? Become someone I'm not? Get a personality transplant? Get some good drugs that keep me focused?"

"You must do everything you say you're going to do for your people, when you say you're going to do it. If you say you'll call tomorrow, you must. If you say you'll get them the documents by Friday, you must move heaven and earth to do that. It's everything. Trust is earned, not just by the big things, but even more so by the little things."

68. Give Power to the Other Person

When I'm getting ready to persuade a person, I spend one-third of the time thinking about myself, what I'm going to say, and two-thirds of the time thinking about him and what he is going to say.
—Abraham Lincoln

When I'm in a leadership position, there's always a hidden fear inside the person I'm leading and about to talk to. If I don't understand that fear, I'm going to have a very hard time creating agreements with that person. And motivation is all about creating agreements.

My goal is to get my people to agree to work with me. I may want them to agree with me to perform at a higher level, or to get some work done that I think needs to be done, or to communicate with me differently, or to treat the customer differently. In all these cases, it's an agreement that I need.

But there's a reason (you know what it is by now...here's a hint: It's fear) why the person on the other side will push back at me and try not to agree with me. And once we understand that reason, we have the ability to create agreements much faster. The focus of my understanding must always be: How do I remove the fear?

Top hypnotists will tell you that they can't even begin to work with a subject whom they can't relax. When a person is not relaxed, she is not open to suggestion, hypnotic or otherwise. Most managers who try to create agreements with other people actually *cause* the fear in the other person to get worse as the conversation goes on.

So how do you create an agreement in such a way that the employee's fear buttons are not being pushed, and he's not pushing back in self-defense? Ask questions, because questions honor the employee's thoughts and feelings. When people fear losing power and balance and they push back (with objections, defensiveness, and so on), it looks like strength! "Well, there's a feisty person! There's a person who knows their own mind. There's a person who's not going to get pushed around." Not true. That's a *scared* person!

People don't want you to sell them on your idea, *they want to sell themselves.* They want it to be *their* idea to do the thing, not yours. That's the secret to motivation, right there.

Let's say you want one of your employees to get forms turned back to you in a more timely manner. If you talk to that employee in an assertive way and say, "You know what, I need to talk to you. I didn't get those forms from you on time." You know what happens? Defensiveness and fear: "There's no *way* I could get them back to you on time because our computer system was down for two days. Actually, our people did pretty well given what was going on here at this office. We did very well, as a matter of fact, and we're doing better than can be expected down here."

Your employee is defending what went on, because your employee is afraid that he will be judged poorly, that he might even be asked to leave the company because he can't get his forms in on time. And all you've done—the only mistake you have made—is you've put something aggressively out there that pushed his button, so you've awakened the fear and caused him to push back.

And if you are clueless about fear and don't know what is going on, you are liable to push even *more* buttons in response to the fear. You might say, "Well you know that computer system was down at another division across town and *they* got theirs in on time."

Now your employee is more frightened, even more anxious.

"Yeah, but they've got a bigger staff than we do. We're understaffed here. Always have been."

The more you push, the more he pushes back. The more defensive you are, the more defensive he is. And, the more defensive he is, the less likely he is to turn those forms in on time next week, which is all you wanted in the first place. It was all you wanted, but it was what you yourself made impossible.

This human push-back dynamic challenges marriages, it slows down careers, and it makes a manager's life a misery. A manager can ask gentle questions and let the people she leads think and speak and make their own fresh commitments. That's how motivation happens.

69. Don't Forget to Breathe

In war, as in peace, a man needs all the brains he can get. Nobody ever had too many brains. Brains come from oxygen. Oxygen comes from the lungs where the air goes when we breathe. The oxygen in the air gets into the blood and travels to the brain. Any fool can double the size of his lungs. —George S. Patton

Scott Richardson recalls the role breathing plays in achieving success as a leader. Yes, breathing, as in, don't forget to breathe.

⌘⌘⌘

Rodney Mercado never actually mentioned it. We never spoke about it, and yet I noticed it, and I copied him and modeled him, because when Mercado played an instrument, he was taking some of the most extraordinarily deep breaths that I'd ever heard a human being take. And so even though he never mentioned it, I figured, if it works for him, I'm going to do the same thing. And since then, I've learned how important breath is to our energy, our focus, and our concentration.

So, I would take a deep breath inward right before I started to play the violin, and then I would breathe out as I was bowing. And then as I changed the bow stroke, I would take another breath and so I would breathe in unison with the music I was performing. I still do this to this day.

Putting so much energy and *intensity* (Mercado's favorite word) into the performance was what produced the result that would move people who heard it.

⌘⌘⌘

As leaders, our own energy and intensity are monitored by our people. They take many of their own subtle psychological cues from how we look: our movements and expressions (or lack of them). This is why we must learn to breathe deeply and lead. To really get out there and lead with enthusiasm. To generate excitement, and then breathe again, even more deeply. The word *inspire* literally means "to breathe in." We don't want to stagnate all day, breathing shallowly behind our desk or in front of our computer. That won't inspire anyone.

70. Know You've Got the Time

Start by doing what's necessary, then what's possible,
and suddenly you are doing the impossible.
—St. Francis

Most managers do small things all day long. They start the day by doing all the easy things. They go through their e-mail over and over again. They ask themselves subconsciously: *What are some little tasks that I can do that aren't difficult? What are things to do that will make it look like I'm being a manager while I figure out what really needs to be done? If anybody were watching me, would they say I am just doing what a manager needs to do? I'm doing what I need to do; these things need to be done sooner or later.*

But a motivational leader has the ability and the opportunity to live life differently, to take the time to live by rational choice of priority instead of feelings, and to leave the infantile behind. The key is taking the time.

The sense that time is getting away, that there's really not enough time in the day, works against this. But you can learn to stay grounded in this fact: We all have 24 hours. It doesn't matter how rich or powerful you are, you still only have 24 hours. Not a minute more. So there's no sense in saying, "I don't have as much time as other people. I'd love to do that but I don't have the time." That's just not true.

Only you can slow time down to the speed of life by choosing what you choose to do. And once you do, it becomes that much easier to motivate and teach others to do the same.

71. Use the Power of Deadlines

> The best way to predict the future is to create it.
>
> —Peter Drucker

Put your requests into a time frame. If there is no pressing time frame, make one up. If you want a report from someone, finish your request by asking, "And may I have this by the end of our business day Thursday?"

Various dictionaries describe a deadline as a time by which something must be done; originally meaning "a line that does not move," and "a line around a military prison beyond which an escaping prisoner *could be shot*." Literally, it is a line over which the person or project becomes dead! Deadlines propel action. So when you want to get people into action, give them a deadline.

If you make a request without including a date or time, then you don't have anything that you can hold the other person accountable for. You have a wished for and hoped for action hanging out there in space with no time involved. People are only motivated when we use both space *and* time. The space-time continuum is a motivator's best friend.

Once, we were leisurely writing a book when the publisher called back to impose a month-away deadline to make the fall catalog for the big Christmas sales season. Then, all of a sudden, we swung into gear, writing and editing 20 hours a day, until we delivered the finished manuscript to our publisher. It turned out to be the best-written book we'd ever done.

Without a deadline, there is no goal, just a nebulous request that adds to the general confusion at work. You will be doing a person a favor by putting your request into a time frame. And if the time is too short, he or she can negotiate it. Let your people participate. It isn't a matter of *who* gets to set the deadline, it's a matter of having one. Either way, it is settled, clear, and complete.

Most managers don't do this. They have hundreds of un-fulfilled requests floating around the workplace, because they aren't prioritized. Those requests keep getting put off. Deadlines will fix all of that.

72. Translate Worry Into Concern

> Difficulties are meant to rouse, not discourage.
> —William Ellery Channing, minister
> and psychologist

Leaders don't help anyone by worrying. Worry is a misuse of their imagination. Practice upgrading your worry to concern. Then, once you state your concern, create your action plan to address it.

If we respond to our problems in life by worrying about them, we will reduce our mood and energy, and lower our self-esteem. Being a *worrier* is hardly a powerful self-concept. It also is not inspiring to others when they see their leader worrying.

Instead of worrying, imagine some action you could take now, something bold and beautiful inspired by the current so-called problem. Getting into that habit raises self-esteem and increases energy levels and concurrently love of life. People are more motivated by people in love with life than by people who worry about life.

73. Let Your Mind Rule Your Heart

> If you don't think about the future,
> you won't have one. —Henry Ford

Managers who approach life as if they're still children, or as adults who are living out their unresolved childhood issues, will not be able to focus on their employees, their customers, or the hunt for great prosperity.

Leadership requires that your logical, problem-solving left brain be in charge of your right brain. It requires a fierce intellect willing to hang in there against all your people's complaints (real and imaginary). It requires a thrill in finding a new route to solutions.

Leadership requires that the chess master in you be in charge of the thinking and decision-making processes throughout the day.

Leadership is about making clear, smart decisions about where and how you spend your time. Leading people is about getting *smarter* with your time every day. The great chess master Kasparov lived by his motto: "Think seven moves ahead."

Intellectually, motivating others is about reverse engineering. You decide what you want, and then you think backward from that. You begin at the end and engineer backward to this fresh moment right now. Always have the end in mind when you approach your team or when you make that phone call. Those people best at motivating others are the ones who are the most conscious of what they're doing. They are the continuous thinkers, and their people appreciate them for it.

As you drive around today, think things through. Think about what you would appreciate most if you were a member of your own team. Think about ways to connect and gain trust. Think. Think about that nice extra touch, that nice little piece of communication you want to make. Think about the questions you want to ask. Think about being a detective. It's a crime that your employee is not performing at her full potential. It's a crime that she is considering leaving the company. Solve that crime.

74. Build a Culture of Acknowledgment

> I have always said that if I were a rich man I'd hire a professional praiser. —Sir Osbert Sitwell, poet

One way to motivate others is to change the question you ask yourself each day. Instead of, *How do I get them to do less of what bothers me?* I might want to change that to, *What is the best thing I can do to get my team to do more of what I want them to do?*

Most managers find out what's wrong, and then criticize it. They look for the problems, and then they say, "You know, we really can't have this. You've got to fix this; this is really not good enough."

But that approach causes resentment on the part of the person who's being criticized. What works better is recognition, acknowledgment, and appreciation. Any way it can be done.

When I'm driving in to work, I tell myself: *I'm deliberately going to build a culture of acknowledgment here—where people feel recognized for every little thing they do. They will feel visible, and they will feel as if they're appreciated and acknowledged. I want them to know that what they do is being seen, is being thought about, and is being celebrated. That is the culture that I will create to grow productivity.*

Whenever possible, I want to recognize those people in front of other people. And if possible, I want to recognize them in front of their families, somehow. Maybe I'll send an award or a note from the company president to the person's home. I want to let that person's family see that he or she is really appreciated.

75. Seize Responsibility

Ninety-nine percent of failures come from people who
have a habit of making excuses.
—George Washington Carver

"I sure wish people would take responsibility around here!" one of the attorneys in Scott Richardson's law firm said to him. "It seems like the people I'm managing are 'pass the buck' artists."

"Well, have you talked to them about what responsibility is?" Scott replied.

"Not really," the attorney said.

"Why not play a little word game with me for a second. I will say a word, and you tell me the first word that pops into your head. Fair enough?"

"Oh boy, here we go."

"No, this will be useful. I promise."

"Okay, shoot. What's the word?

"What's the first word that comes to mind when you hear the word *responsibility*?

"Obligation," said the attorney.

"Great," said Scott. "Now let's break down the word *responsibility* into its component parts. It literally is response *ability* or the ability to respond. The ability to do something! Responsible is response-able, or being able to respond. That's all responsibility is. Responsibility doesn't have anything to do with obligation or the host of other negative words that are associated with it, words that have an intimidating connotation, such as obligation, burden, debt, fault, and so on. If you want your people to take responsibility, you need to be clear yourself and with them that responsibility doesn't have anything to do with those other words. It is simply the ability to respond, the ability to do something. Just tell your people you believe in them. That you know they have the ability to respond to this challenge, and you support them in doing so."

Steve Hardison is a life coach extraordinaire we've worked with and written about extensively in previous books. Hardison was invited to attend a board meeting of a company he was considering coaching. The first item on the agenda was: "Whose fault is it that we have a $100,000 computer system that is a piece of junk?"

The president turned to one of the vice presidents and said, "Joe, this is all your fault!" Joe quickly responded, "No, it's not. I didn't draw up the specs. John did!" John quickly responded, "Hey, wait a minute. I didn't choose the vendor. Rose did." Rose said, "Hey, that wasn't really my decision, I just gave my recommendation to you!"

And so the people at the board meeting just kept passing the buck around and around the board room.

Finally, Coach Hardison motioned to the CEO and interrupted the conversation.

"Can I say something?" he asked the CEO.

"Sure, what?"

"I am responsible for the computer system." announced Hardison.

"What?" shot back the CEO. "We don't even know who you are! Why would you say anything so crazy?"

"Well," said Hardison, "someone needs to be responsible!"

"Oh, yeah," replied the CEO.

Once Hardison had taken responsibility for the computer system, he was able to lead the discussion on how to move forward and solve the problem. This is true response-ability rather than responsibility = blame.

Another one of our affiliate coaches started as a salesperson at a high-tech company. In less than two years, he was the CEO. When he was asked how he did it, he said, "I considered it *my company* from day one. If I saw a piece of paper on the floor, I either picked it up or got someone to do it. If there was a division of the company that was not working, I got involved and got it running better, even though technically it had nothing to do with my job. After a while, they asked me to be the CEO, but I had already taken responsibility for the entire company long before."

So if you would like to be the CEO someday, start from this moment, taking 100-percent responsibility for the entire company. Nothing will motivate your people more than that.

76. Get Some Coaching Yourself

A teacher affects eternity. He can never tell where his influence stops. —Henry B. Adams, American historian

Great coaches always cite the coaches they themselves learned from. In today's environment, most top business leaders have coaches—personal success coaches or life coaches who take them to higher levels of success than they ever could have attained on their own.

The object of the coaching process is to allow the leader to discover his or her hidden strengths and to bring this person to the forefront in the daily life of the business. Every great actor, dancer, and athlete credits most of their career progress to a coach who gave them support and teaching along the way. In the past, our society celebrated the concept of coaching in sports and show business, because those were fields where excellence was always expected. Business was just business.

Now, because of the growth of coaching, today's business leader has the same opportunity to explore the upper limits of his or her excellence as does an athlete or an actor. Coaching makes that opportunity a conscious part of the leader's career. "I absolutely believe that people, unless coached, never reach their maximum capabilities," said Bob Nardelli, former CEO of Home Depot. If you're a leader, be open to being coached. There's no value in going it alone just to prove you can.

77. Make It Happen Today

What would be the use of immortality to a person who cannot use well a half an hour?
—Ralph Waldo Emerson

The ability to motivate others flows from the importance that we attach to today. What can we do *today*?

John Wooden was the most successful college basketball coach of all time. His UCLA teams won 10 national championships in a 12-year time span. Wooden created a major portion of his coaching and living philosophy from one thought— a single sentence passed on to him by his father when Wooden was a little boy: "Make each day your masterpiece."

While other coaches would try to gear their players toward important games in the future, Wooden always focused on today. His practice sessions at UCLA were every bit as important as any championship game. In his philosophy, there was no reason not to make today the proudest day of your life. There was no reason not to play as hard in practice as you do in a game. He wanted every player to go to bed each night thinking, Today, I was at my best.

Most of us, however, don't want to live this way. The future is where our happiness lies, so we live in the future. The past is where the problem began, so we live in the past. But every good thing that ever happened, happened now, right now. Leadership takes place now, too.

The key to leading others is in your willingness to do important things—but to do them now. Today is your whole life in miniature. You were "born" when you woke up, and you'll "die" when you go to sleep. It was designed this way, so that you could live your whole life in a day. Do you still want to walk around telling your team you're having a bad day? When your people see you making each day your masterpiece they will pick it up as a way to live and work.

78. Learn the Inner Thing

Your vision will become clear only when you can look into your own heart. Whoever looks outside only dreams, whoever looks inside also awakens.

—Carl Jung

Most managers and leaders in this country subconsciously use a Western model of macho warfare for leadership. It is an ineffective model.

Scott studied kung fu in Taiwan, and his instructor taught him about inner forces in every human being that can be called on to achieve great things. As Scott rose to prominence as an attorney and a consultant, he credited his martial arts training for much of his insight.

⌘⌘⌘

Scott recalls: When I was in Taiwan and the United States, I saw demonstrations of kung fu masters who, for instance, set up three candles. They had a piece of clear glass in between their face and the candles, so they couldn't blow on the candles. And they proceeded to, in what looked like slow motion, move their fist toward the flame, and from a distance of at least 12 inches, put out these flames. One of my friends who was a black belt in karate watched a demonstration with me. He turned to me and said, "Scott, you've studied kung fu, haven't you?" And I said, "A little bit." And he said, "How do they do that? I'm a black belt in karate and one of our tests is we have to be able to put out a candle flame with our strongest kick. We can come as close to the candle flame as we can, and I had to train hours and hours to do that. It's physically impossible to do it from 12 inches away with the strongest kick I have. I could never do it with a slow motion punch. How do those guys do it?"

I replied, "Well, actually it's based on something called *ki*."

I can extend ki, change my body posture slightly, and be practicing the advanced martial art of aikido.

So with any activity involving a physical body, you can be practicing a version of this martial art aikido. The basic principles of extending ki include focusing on your one point and thinking about that. In aikido, they teach you that if you focus your attention on your one point, which is a point 2 inches below your navel, you automatically are centered.

That's all you have to do. You can do it in a team meeting. You can do it during a one-on-one performance review. There's no great mystery about it.

The aikido instructor does a demonstration in which he says, "Okay, focus on your one point," and he presses on your chest, and you don't fall over, you're very centered and strong. And then he lightly slaps you on the top of your head with one hand while he pushes on your chest with the other, and you immediately fall over backwards.

And he says, "What just happened? You had your awareness on your one point and, when you did, I couldn't push you over. And then as soon as I slapped you on the top of your head, what happened? Your awareness went up there to your head and I pushed you over without even trying."

I did this simple demonstration to my father—the world's biggest skeptic—and he said, "There must be a physical explanation for it." But there was not. He hadn't moved a muscle in his body! Nothing physical. Just his focus. And that was the difference between his being grounded and centered and strong, and then losing focus.

⌘⌘⌘

Most people in the workplace are not centered. They live off the top of their head where, basically, anything that comes up in life is going to tip them over. Tip them off center. As their leader, you can model being centered. You can radiate the immovable lifeforce, the ki inside everyone. In your next managerial challenge, try relaxing and allowing a force greater than yourself to flow through you and then out into the situation. And it won't be long before you, too, are a legend in your organization, simply for being centered.

79. Forget About Failure

A life spent making mistakes is not only more honorable but more useful than a life spent in doing nothing.
—George Bernard Shaw

Leaders of highly productive teams, especially at the beginning of their careers, obsess about failure. They take a bad conversation with a problem employee very personally. They get hurt. They get depressed. They get angry and start hating their profession.

But soon they see that failure is just an outcome. It is not bad or good, just neutral. It can be turned into something good if it's studied for the wisdom to be gained from it. And it can be turned into something bad if it is made into something personal.

The great professor of linguistics S.I. Hayakawa used to say that there were basically two kinds of people: the kind of person who fails at something and says, "I failed at that," and the person who fails at something and says, "I'm a failure." The first person is in touch with the truth, and the second person is not.

"I'm a failure!"

That claim doesn't always appear to the outsider to be a lie. It can look like a sad form of self-acceptance. In fact, we can even associate such exaggerating with truthful confession: "Why not admit it? I'm a failure." But in psychological terms, what we're hearing is the voice of fear. It's the opposite of a voice of purpose; it is a voice of surrender, internal defeat, quitting before I begin. (Defeat and failure on the external can actually be refreshing and rejuvenating. The great football coach Woody Hayes used to say, "Nothing cleanses the soul like getting the hell kicked out of you.")

As you lead people today, always keep in mind this one true fact: There is nothing wrong with them. They have it inside themselves to prosper and excel as professionals. Get connected to that truth and show your people how to leave all their "I'm a failure" thoughts in the trash where they belong.

80. Follow Consulting With Action

Action is eloquence. —Shakespeare

Scott has been practicing law for more than 20 years, had his own law firm for 17 years, and even owned another law firm, which he sold during that time. He has also had up to 15 employees, and coached other lawyers and executives.

He states: There's no question in my mind that it is one thing to be a coach, another thing to be in the role of the CEO. I think the perspective of being the one in the hot seat, so to speak, is extremely valuable. Having been both roles, I have coached and been coached, I know a coach can be absolutely invaluable to the person in the hot seat. But you can bring in the world's greatest coach and if the person in the hot seat still chooses, for whatever reason, not to take the coaching, then the effort is lost.

That's the reason why CEOs are the most important people in the organization, because they can choose not to make things happen as well as to make things happen. A coach is not going to wave a magic wand and cause things to change regardless of that decision. It can't work that way. In the end, a coach can only shine a light and assist. It's always the willingness of the CEO to generate the action that makes a true difference. So if you are getting coaching, follow it up with action. Massive action. To do so will be eloquent.

81. Create a Vision

> The reason most major goals are not achieved is that we spend our time doing second things first.
> —Robert J. McKain, management consultant

Without creating a vision for my team, my team will live according to its problems. Without goals (the subsets of vision), my team will just fight fires, work through emotional upsets, and worry about the dysfunctional behavior of other people. I, as their leader, will have attracted a problem-based existence.

Soon, I will only end up doing what I *feel* like doing, which will sell me short and draw on the smallest of my brain's resources. But when we begin to *create*, we use more of the brain. We rise up to our highest functioning as humans. So it's my primary job as a motivator to create a vision of who we want to be, and then live in that picture as if it were already happening in this very moment. It has to be a vision I can talk about every day. It can't be a framed statement on the wall that no one can relate to after some company retreat is over. It is not surprising that one of the biggest complaints about leaders that show up on employee surveys is, "He had no idea where we were headed. He had no vision of our future that he could tell us about."

Create a vision. Live the vision.

82. Stop Looking Over Your Shoulder

Courage is not the absence of fear, but rather the judgment that something else is more important than fear. —Ambrose Redmoon, American philosopher

The worst trap for you as a leader is to begin anticipating what your own leaders think of you from moment to moment, to do superficial things to impress upper management, rather than doing real things to encourage your people. Great leadership-by-example (the ultimate motivator of others) comes from getting better at what you do independently, and not living in anticipation of other people's opinions of you. It allows you to increase your leadership strength every day, and to build your self-esteem.

Paradoxically, the more we focus on doing our own best work and staying in action to fulfill our personal and professional goals, the more help we are to others. It's hardly selfish. There's no one less motivational to be around than someone who is always trying to anticipate the criticisms of others.

83. Lead by Selling

> Everyone lives by selling something.
> —Robert Louis Stevenson

Dan Kennedy is a local marketing expert who has done a lot of direct sales in his lifetime. He has made the observation that the most successful doctors, lawyers, teachers, and business people that he works with invariably have some sales background.

⌘⌘⌘

Scott recalls: I was wondering why I've never had a problem in enrolling people in projects. It's just been very easy for me, always. And when I heard Dan Kennedy's observation, I thought, *You know, he's right!* Before I had had some direct sales experience, I was very poor at enrolling people in projects and ideas. Afterward, I was great. So let me tell you how I experienced that transformation in my life.

Before I went to college, I decided to spend a summer selling books door-to-door in Pennsylvania. I attended a week-long sales training school put on by a company called Southwestern, the largest door-to-door book sales company in the United States. (They primarily used college students to work during the summer.)

During this week, we learned our basics. It was the old-style selling: You learned your sales pitch, memorized it. Then you learned about door approaches, how to inspire confidences and get in and make your presentation, and how to close (gracefully asking for the order). Just classic selling.

The very first house I called on, I actually sold something. And I thought, *Man, this stuff really works. This is a piece of cake.* That was the only sale I had for two weeks. And so my sales manager decided to start working with me to see what wasn't working. He gave me a diagnosis: "Scott, you're not closing. You're not even asking for the sale."

"What do you mean I'm not closing? Of course, I'm closing."

"No, you're not. You didn't close once."

"I didn't?"

"No. Look, I know we taught you to close at least three times, but for you there's no limit. Just start off showing them a little bit about the books, then you close. And if they say, 'No, I'm not interested,' you say, 'I know just what you mean,' and you show them a little bit more, and you close again."

So I said, "That's crazy. They're going to throw me out on my butt!"

"Just try it."

Well, I figured the other way wasn't working, so what the heck?

So the next house we called on, I presented the books a little bit and asked the lady for the order. She said, "Well, I'm really not interested."

"That's fine, I know exactly what you mean," I said.

Then I showed her a little bit more and closed her again. And she said, "Well, I don't know, I don't have the money."

"I know exactly what you mean," I said.

And I showed her a little bit more and closed her again. I closed her at least five times and I thought, *Man, how long is this going to take? I guess she hasn't kicked me out, so I'll keep going.*

And finally, I think on the sixth close, she said, "Okay!"

I was shocked.

Later on, something very surprising happened.

It turned out that this nice lady worked in a bank right there in Gettysburg, Pennsylvania. One day, when I went to the bank to bring all my checks from my sales to deposit, I saw her there. She was working as a teller. I put my checks in to deposit, and she seemed very embarrassed to see me. So I thought, *Oh my gosh, maybe I just ramrodded her into buying and now she feels bad. But oh well, we always tell them they can cancel the order.*

So I shoved my checks toward her and said, "I want to deposit these checks."

And she said, "You know, Scott, I hope you didn't mind that I took so long to decide, but I just wanted to make sure that I really wanted those books. Now I'm so glad I bought them."

What a lesson. So from then on, I've never been afraid to ask. In terms of leadership, this simply means asking for what you want, being very direct with your requests, and having your communication centered on requests and promises.

⌘⌘⌘

Figure out what you want your people to buy into. Then sell them on the idea. But don't forget to close them. Don't forget to make a strong, specific request (the close), and then receive a strong, specific promise in return.

84. Hold on to Principle

> In matters of style, swim with the current;
> In matters of principle, stand like a rock.
> —Thomas Jefferson

"Discipline yourself, and others won't need to," Coach John Wooden would tell his players. "Never lie. Never cheat. Never steal," and "Earn the right to be proud and confident."

We're starting to learn why John Wooden was the most successful college basketball coach of all time. No one has ever even come close. No one has ever motivated his athletes so superbly as Wooden.

Rick Reilly, the talented sportswriter, recalls:

If you played for him, you played by his rules: Never score without acknowledging a teammate. One word of profanity, and you're done for the day. Treat your opponent with respect. Coach Wooden believed in hopelessly out-of-date stuff that never did anything but win championships. No dribbling behind the back or through the legs. ("There's no need," he'd say.) No UCLA basketball number was retired under his watch. ("What about the fellows who wore that number before? Didn't they contribute to the team?" Coach Wooden would say.) No long hair, no facial hair. ("They take too long to dry, and you could catch cold leaving the gym," he'd say.) That one drove his players bonkers. One day, All-America center Bill Walton showed up with a full beard. "It's my right," he insisted. Wooden asked if he believed that strongly. Walton said he did. "That's good, Bill," Coach said. "I admire people who have strong beliefs and stick by them, I really do. We're going to miss you." Walton shaved it right then and there. Now Walton calls once a week to tell Coach he loves him.

You have two ways to go as a motivator of others. You can seek to be liked or you can, as John Wooden did, earn their respect. When their respect runs deep enough, you may end up being loved.

85. Create Your Relationships

A life of reaction is a life of slavery, intellectually, and spiritually. One must fight for a life of action, not reaction. —Rita Mae Brown, mystery author

When we are coaching leaders who are having a tough time motivating others, it always becomes apparent that their basic problem is that they're *reacting* to their people all day long.

They're wallowing in their own negative emotional reactions to people. After a while, in listening to these types of managers, we get a funny impression that we're listening to the words of country music. You know those country songs we're talking about. The themes are: "I've been hurt so many times, I'm never going to reach out again," or "I don't trust women," or "You can't trust men." Actual songs have titles such as "Is It Cold in Here or Is it You?" or "My Wife Ran Away with My Best Friend and I Miss Him."

Country music in and of itself is great, and the really sad songs—the ones that express the poetry of victimization—are beautiful in their own way, but their basic philosophy is not an effective way to create the motivated team we want.

Managers who go through their days reacting emotionally to the behavior of their people truly are miserable. What those managers need is a gentle shift. Not a huge change, but a shift, just like the gentle shift of gears in a finely tuned car. They need to shift from reacting to creating. All of this reacting they do has become a habit, and because it's only a habit, it's completely open to a shift.

Business coach Dan Sullivan nails it when he says, "The difficulty in changing habits lies in the fact that we are changing something that feels completely natural to us. Good habits feel natural; bad habits feel natural. That is the nature of a habit. When you change a bad habit that feels natural to a good habit that feels natural, you feel exactly the same. It is just that you get completely different results."

One of the first steps on the path out of the habit of reacting to the people we manage is to ask ourselves a simple question. It was a question first asked by Ralph Waldo Emerson many years ago: "Why should my happiness depend on the thoughts going on in someone else's head?"

This question, no matter how we answer it in any given moment, gives us the mental perspective we need to start seeing the possibilities for creatively relating to others instead of just reacting to them.

86. Don't Be Afraid to Make Requests

As you enter positions of trust and power, dream a little before you think. —Toni Morrison, author

Don't you wish you could just *ask* your superiors to help your team do certain things? It would make leadership much simpler if it could become a matter of requests and promises and follow-through action. It can. It will help you to know, before you ask, that everyone (your superiors, your customers, your employees) really wants to say yes.

We once took a seminar ourselves on communication, and one of the exercises they gave us was designed to dramatize this fact that people really want to say yes.

They gave us an assignment over a long dinner break to go out and make three unreasonable requests to get people to say no. That was the assignment: You *had* to get three no responses before you came back.

We thought it would be simple. After Scott finished dinner, he went over to a lady at the next table and said, "You know, ma'am, I'm a little short on cash, would you mind picking up my meal?" He figured that was a pretty unreasonable request and he was sure she'd tell him to get lost.

He was stunned when she didn't say that. "Well, I'm not sure I have enough money to cover that right now," she said, so Scott began coaching her to say no.

"Oh, that's okay, just asking. You can say no."

And she wouldn't say no! She said, "Well, I'm not sure...."

"In other words, no?"

"Well, I guess not. No."

"Thanks!"

Scott had to work very hard just to get her to say no. Then when Scott walked over to the cashier to pay for the meal, there was a man who was waiting there and Scott thought, *No problem. I'll get a quick no from him.*

"You know, I'm a little short on cash," Scott said. "Would you mind picking up my bill?"

"Well, I'm not sure. What's this about?"

"Well, you can say no."

It took him quite a while (soon Scott was begging him for a no) but he finally got him to say no.

Two down, one to go. So Scott turned to the lady right next to him and said, "How about you? Would you pick up my bill?" She had just heard what went on, so it didn't look like it would be too hard! But it was. And after a very long negotiation, after she was quite willing to pay for his meal, she said no.

That one exercise taught us a lot. People all want to say yes.

So now, whenever we have a project that we want to create, we feel free to go out there and start asking. We don't have any fear or hesitancy in making what most people would call unreasonable requests. Because we know from experience (after having it verified many times over) that people's natural tendency is to say yes.

So, ask for what you want, both up and down the pecking order. If your team needs something from the higher-ups, go ask for it. When you get their agreements keep bringing in good news for your team about what the top people are agreeing to do to move things forward. You'll be teaching them the power of requests.

87. Don't Change Yourself

It takes a tremendous act of courage to admit to yourself that you are not defective in any way whatsoever.
—Cheri Huber, author/Zen philosopher

A lot of people who hear our talks or read our books contact us for coaching, saying, "I really need to make a change. I need to totally change my life. I have been an unconscious,

bossy, paranoid manager and I'm ready to learn to be a leader."
We tell them what we tell everyone: You don't need to change.
All you need is a gentle shift.

To get your sports car to send itself into a smoother, faster
speed, do you need to take out the gearbox and put in a new
one? Or do you simply need to shift gears? When you do shift
gears, is it hard to do? Hard, like changing a tire? Or do you
just slide into it? For your mind to take you to the next level of
leadership performance, all you need to do is shift gears. You
don't need to replace your gear box. Just shift. And then zoom.
Zoom. Just like that.

Do you need to change your attitude? How? Why? What is
an attitude anyway? How do you change it? *Attitude* is a word
that old people use to intimidate young people. It's the ultimate
sadistic control device: "You better change your attitude, son!"

"How, Dad?"

"Don't mess with me, son."

"What is attitude, Dad? How do I access it? How do I even
identify it, much less change it?"

"It's poor, I can tell you that."

If you were ever part of such a conversation, you got off on
the wrong track in this whole concept of change. Reinventing
yourself happens. But it happens as a result of a series of gentle
shifts. It's a path, not a revolution. It becomes a way of life.

Just begin.

88. Pump Up Your E-mails

No pessimist ever discovered the secrets of the stars,
or sailed to an uncharted land, or opened a new
heaven to the human spirit. —Helen Keller

Every e-mail communication you send to your team is an opportunity. It's a fresh chance to energize that team and spread the optimism you want to fuel the contagious enthusiasm your next project needs. But nine out of 10 managers ignore this opportunity. Instead, they often send neutral e-mails, or short, terse e-mails...sometimes even angry e-mails. Those are all mistakes. Because your first job, even before your job of informing others, is to motivate others.

So let's begin here: Realize that e-mail is a cold medium anyway. There is no voice tone in it. There is no twinkle in the eye or warmth of expression. It's just cold, electronic type. Therefore, even a neutral e-mail feels chilly to the recipient. Even a simple transfer of information feels icy and negative, unless you seize the opportunity to pump it up. Always pump it up.

Every communication from a manager to an employee is an opportunity to instill optimism. Don't waste that opportunity. A true leader never does. Look at your e-mail before you send it. Is it uplifting? Does it contain an acknowledgement or an appreciation of the recipient? Does it praise the recipient? Does it inspire? Is it going to make someone happy?

If not, take the extra minute to go back over it. Change the negative tone to a positive one. Brighten it up. Ask yourself: *Would I be happy to get this e-mail? Would I feel honored and appreciated if I received it?*

Behavioral studies continue to show that positive reinforcement works more than seven times better than negative criticism to change behavior. Negative criticism causes resentment, depression, anger, and sabotage. People will sabotage your leadership if they feel alienated and underappreciated.

Pump things up and watch what happens. Don't take this on faith; use trial and error. Send half of your people a neutral e-mail and half a positive one, and see which gets the best results. You will be able to test this concept by doing it. You will be delighted with the results you get.

89. Stop Pushing

Pull the string, and it will follow wherever you wish.
Push it, and it will go nowhere at all.
—Dwight D. Eisenhower

Thomas Crum gives seminars on how to use aikido philosophy in daily business life. He calls what he teaches, "the magic of conflict." Scott remembers being there during one of the demonstrations Crum gave. Crum had someone come to the front of the room and stand up in front of him.

"Put out your hand, like this," said Crum as he put his hand up as if taking an oath, touching the student's upraised hand. The student just naturally, automatically reacted by pushing back.

Crum said, "That's the natural way of human beings. I push, you give me resistance. You push back."

Then he asked the student to extend his hand in the form of a fist. He did, and then Tom Crum put his hand in a closed fist in front of him and they both pushed against each other, each fist pushing the other.

"This is the way we experience life a lot," said Crum. "Just like this. A stalemate or struggle, where I'm trying to win or you're trying to win. In aikido, we don't ever resist."

Right at that moment, Crum dropped his fist down, and instantly the volunteer pushed right by him (and, in aikido, you turn in the direction of the person going by you). Crum turned with the volunteer and guided him quickly and gently to the floor.

Crum said, "Now, this is aikido. I no longer resist, so we're no longer fighting. And guess what? We're in perfect alignment, so it's very easy for me to direct this person wherever I choose him to go. And that's how aikido works."

In fact, the words *ai ki do* mean "blending our inner forces," not force against force. And every move in aikido comes to that point, where both the aggressor's ki and my ki are blended. Right at that point, when we're in alignment, I have control over the other person and what happens to him and his body. Totally. It takes no effort. Because we're in complete alignment.

The application to motivating others is profound, because I don't really want to resist what my people are doing or saying. I want to guide their natural inner energy toward a mutual goal—theirs and mine. I want to receive and guide my people's natural energy...I don't want to oppose it or make it wrong.

90. Become Conscious

*A boss creates fear, a leader, confidence. A boss fixes
blame, a leader corrects mistakes. A boss knows all, a
leader asks questions. A boss makes work drudgery, a
leader makes it interesting.*
—Russell H. Ewing, author

If I'm an unconscious manager, can I be taught to be a true
leader?

Of course I can. If you are going to turn me into a true
leader, you begin by making what is unconscious (my commitments and operating principles as a leader) become conscious
and clear. That's step one. That process is as simple as teaching
me how to use a computer program.

Perhaps you hold a leadership meeting and state very clearly why and how you intend to lead. You make everything clear.
If there are other leaders in the room, even leaders whom you
lead, you invite them to do the same. The more open we all are
about how we intend to lead, the more motivated our people
will be.

One of the exercises we like to do in our leadership seminars is to ask people to write down the name of someone in
their lives whom they admired and respected as a leader. It may
be their grandmother, an old platoon leader, or a former teacher,
or a manager from a company they used to work for. Some
people write down a leader in history that had an influence on
them, such as John F. Kennedy or Winston Churchill.

You might want to do this exercise right now. Think of
someone in your own life you respected as a leader. Jot the name
down. Now, write three qualities about that person that you
admired the most. Don't read on until you do.

Okay, now look at those three qualities. They may be anything—honesty, openness, a total belief in you, creativity, non-judgmental teaching style—whatever the three qualities were, look at them. More than likely, and more than nine times out of 10, these are qualities *you have* as a leader. And these are the three things your people would say about *you!* Look at them. Is it not true? Are they not who you are?

This is a powerful exercise because it shows you how you have already internalized and already modeled the leaders you admired. But until now, it has been subconscious. The trick is to make it conscious, and be very awake to it every day.

There is nothing so disheartening as a leader's having a per-ceived hidden agenda, which comes from overly unconscious values at play. It discourages your people when they have to guess where you're coming from every day.

Far better to have both you and your people fully *conscious* of what you stand for.

91. Come From the Future

> The very essence of leadership is that you have to have vision. You can't blow an uncertain trumpet.
> —Theodore M. Hesburgh, Former president, Notre Dame

Managers often, quite unconsciously, allow team meetings and one-on-one conferences to focus excessively on the past. But the constant refrain of how things used to be and why things were "easier back then" demoralizes the team. The team sits through unnecessarily long periods of time spent hashing out, venting, and reviewing breakdowns and mistakes. This is done at the expense of the future. It is also done at the expense of optimism and morale and a sense of good, orderly direction.

A good motivator will not make the mistake of obsessively focusing on the past. A good motivator will use the past as a springboard that immediately leads to a discussion of the future: "What can we learn from that mistake that will serve us in the future? And if this happens again, how might we handle it better?"

To a good motivator, the past really has only one purpose: to provide building material for creating the future. The past is not used as something to get hung up on, or an excuse for regret, placing blame, nostalgia, personal attacks, and having a defeated attitude. A leader knows that leadership *means* leading people into the future. Just as a scout leader leads scouts into the woods, a true leader leads team members into the future.

Your shift to better leadership might include learning to make an ever-increasing percentage of your communication focus on the future: discussing your next week, planning your next month, designing your goals for next year, and looking at the opportunities that will be there two years from now. Be thorough and well-prepared when it comes to discussing the future. If the details are not always known, the commitments and vision and strategies are.

Unmotivational managers will unconsciously disown and spread fear about the future. They will say how unpredictable and dangerous the future is. They will exaggerate potential problems and stress the unpredictability of everything. They will attempt to come across as realists, when in fact, it's much more truthful to say that they simply haven't done their home-work. You'll be motivating others to the degree that you are a constant source of information and interesting communication about the future of the team.

92. Teach Them to Teach Themselves

> If you want a man to be for you, never let him feel he
> is dependent on you. Make him feel you are in some
> way dependent on him.
> —General George C. Marshall

Scott remembers a story that Mr. Mercado told him about the great virtuoso Jascha Heifetz and the terribly difficult Tchaikovsky violin concerto.

⌘⌘⌘

Heifetz's teacher was the great German violinist Leopold Auer. Mercado once said, "Auer himself could not play the Tchaikovsky violin concerto up to speed. It'd never been performed up to speed before Heifetz."

Heifetz was the first one to perform this piece up to speed! And if Auer, his teacher, could not perform it up to speed, and he was teaching Heifetz, how then was Heifetz able to do it?

Some people might say, "Well, he was just a talent."

But that wasn't the explanation according to Mr. Mercado. He said, "Scott, if Auer was only teaching Heifetz how to play like Auer, then Heifetz would have never performed that Tchaikovsky violin concerto up to speed. But that isn't what Auer was doing. He was *teaching him how to teach himself* how to play the instrument. And that's how he learned to become better than his teacher."

This is a very powerful distinction. And that really is why Auer was such an extraordinary teacher.

Your goal is to teach as Leopold Auer taught, absolutely unafraid of the people you lead being better than you are, because that's what great coaches and leaders do. They don't teach us how to have a great career. They teach us *how to teach ourselves* how to have a great career.

⌘⌘⌘

93. Stop Apologizing for Change

If the rate of change on the outside exceeds the rate of change on the inside, the end is near.

—Jack Welch

Managers who apologize for any and all changes the team must accommodate are sowing the seeds of low morale and discouragement. Every time they introduce a new policy, product, system, rule, or project, they apologize for it. They imply that change is harmful to the well-being of the team and that change is something we would hope someday to not have to suffer so much of. This is done with the unconscious motive of seeming compassionate and being liked, but it results in creating a team of victims, and it dramatically lengthens the time it takes for the team to assimilate and become comfortable with a change.

A true leader does not apologize for change. A true leader does not feed into the fear that so easily accompanies change. Instead, the leader is an advocate for change. A leader continuously communicates the benefits of an ever-changing organization. A leader endorses an organization that is continuously reinventing itself to higher and higher levels of productivity and innovation.

Every change is made for a reason. Every change was decided upon because the positives of the change outweigh the negatives. So, if you wish to be a highly motivational leader, you simply learn the positives, through and through. You find out everything there is to know about the upside of the change, because that's what leadership is. Leadership is communication of the upside.

Unconscious managers are often as uncomfortable with changes as their own people are, so they constantly apologize for them, which furthers the impression that the team is disconnected completely from the mission of the company. But not you. You are a leader, and so you will always reconnect the team to the mission of the company. Change will not be apologized for. Why apologize for something that will improve the strength of the organization? Every change is made (every last one of them) for the sole purpose of strengthening the ultimate viability of the organization. That's why you advocate the change. That's why you sell it to your team.

94. Let People Find It

> People ask the difference between a leader and a
> boss. The leader works in the open, and the boss in
> covert. The leader leads and the boss drives.
> —Theodore Roosevelt

Scott again recalls coach and teacher Rodney Mercado and his master key to getting remarkable performances out of the people he taught and motivated:

⌘⌘⌘

If you heard any two students of Mercado's play side by side, you would absolutely swear that they did not have the same teacher. You would say it was physically impossible because their playing styles were so radically different. Most people who take music lessons are aware that listeners can identify who a student's teacher is by how the student plays.

But with Mercado, not only could you not do that, but you would absolutely swear that they *couldn't* have the same teacher, that it just couldn't be possible. How did he accomplish that? For one thing, he never told us "don't," he never said "no," and he never told us *how* to play the instrument.

A typical example, a very fundamental thing, was how to hold the bow. He would say, "Okay, Scott, what I'd like you to do is to try holding your hand this way," and he'd have me adopt an extreme position, like holding my hand as far to the right as I possibly could while still being able to use my bow. He'd have me play some music that way, and then say, "Okay, fine. Now I'd like you to do the opposite," and he'd have me put my hand all the way to the left, as far as I could possibly put it—a very uncomfortable position—and then he'd say, "Play this passage."

He would then ask, "Now, if you had to choose one of those two extremes, which one would you choose?"

"Well, all the way to the left, because it's a little less cumbersome than all the way to the right."

"So what that's telling you, Scott, is that you probably want to hold your hand position somewhere between all the way to the right and all the way to the left, and it's probably going to be more to the left than to the right. Find the way that works the best for you."

And if I said, "Well, what if other people say you have to hold your hand a certain way?"

Mercado would then reel off a number of examples of professional violinists who did it differently. He's ask me to reason it out.

"So what is that telling you, Scott?"

"Well, that there isn't one right way to do it."

"Right, so find what works for you."

And that was his teaching method.

So, I learned from that, and when motivating people, I adapted it to mean that there is never one right way to do something. Rather than showing my people the "right way" to make a phone call, or gather information from a client, I will let them develop their own ways. The lesson learned for me way back in music class was that people will motivate *themselves* in their own way if you gently guide them in that direction.

⌘⌘⌘

95. Be a Ruthless Optimist

> A leader is a dealer in hope.
> —Napoleon Bonaparte

Pessimism is the most fundamental of all the mistakes managers can make. It is a position, a pose, taken by the manager of not being optimistic about the future of the organization and, therefore, the future of the team. It is a refusal to prepare for team meetings by learning the rationale behind the latest company decisions. It is a refusal to take a stand for the success of the enterprise. It is a refusal to be an advocate for the organization's ongoing strategy.

It is also an exaggerated tendency to acknowledge and agree with every issue's downside without standing up for the upside. Sometimes optimism is a lonely and courageous position to take, which is why most managers don't do it. The sad thing is, it is what the team wants and needs the most from its leader.

Whereas the unconscious manager doesn't realize what he or she is doing by being so pessimistic all the time, a true leader knows exactly what optimism is and what it is for: Optimism is the practice of focusing on opportunities and possibilities rather than complaints and regrets.

A true optimist is not a brainless Pollyanna wearing rose-colored glasses. A true optimist is more realistic than that. A true optimist is unafraid of confronting and understanding the problems in the organization. But once a problem is fully identified and understood, the optimist returns the thinking to opportunity and possibility.

Optimistic leaders acknowledge the downside of every situation, then focus the majority of their thinking on the upside. They also focus the majority of their communication on the upside. They know that the downside is always well-known throughout the team. But the upside is never as well-known. Who wants to look like an idiotic optimist? It is far more popular and easy to be a clever and witty pessimist. But it is not leadership.

Optimism in the face of a grumbling and pessimistic team takes courage and energy. It is something most team members would never be willing to do. It is the heart and soul of leadership. And while you may be attacked for it now and then, in the end, it is what your team members will love you for the most.

96. Pay Attention

Do not hope wholly to reason away your troubles; do not feed them with attention, and they will die imperceptibly away. Fix your thoughts upon your business, fill your intervals with company, and sunshine will again break in upon your mind.

—Samuel Johnson

Anything you pay attention to expands. It grows. Pay attention to your house plants and they grow. Pay attention to your favorite cause, and your passion and knowledge will grow the success of that cause. Attention is like that. Anywhere you direct it, the object of that attention grows.

When you talk to members of your team, keep paying attention to the end results you want, not the effort to achieve them. When you praise your managers, pay attention to results they achieved that you wanted, not the trying, the effort, or the attempt to do it. Most managers miss this vital point: they keep rewarding the trying, not realizing that doing so sends the subconscious message that trying is always enough. Their people soon think that if they can show they're making efforts, if they can show activity, then there won't be so much focus on end results.

Make sure you reward end results more than anything else. If you do so, you'll get better end results. *You* have to be the one who keeps talking numbers if you want that person to hit his numbers. If, instead, you commiserate with how hard everything is, and you acknowledge how hard everyone is trying, then that's what you'll get: fewer results and more trying. Whatever you praise, grows. Always. It's the law of the harvest.

Attention is powerful. Yet most people allow their attention to be pushed and pulled around all day long by outside forces. A chance phone call. Some annoying e-mail. Somebody walking by their desk and asking a loaded question. Attention gets spread too thinly this way. But your attention is like money. It is a precious treasure. It is paid into things. We say *pay* attention for a reason. It is invested. It gets paid into whatever you choose to pay it into. If you pay it into the things you want (measurable, numerical outcomes and specific results), you will get more and more of what you want.

97. Create a Routine

Patience and perseverance have a magical effect before which difficulties disappear and obstacles vanish.
—John Quincy Adams

Leadership success is not easy, but it is not all that hard, either. It is not nearly as hard as we often make it for ourselves. The major psychological obstacle to motivational success is the myth of permanent characteristics. It is people who think that their habits of action are not habits, but permanent traits. Believing in that totally false myth traps people in a prison, an iron web of limitation. And it's all unnecessary!

The repeated action patterns that you and I demonstrate throughout the day are a result of habit, not the result of permanent characteristics, or character defects, or personality quirks. If we don't like a certain tendency we have (let's say, to procrastinate having that important talk with an employee who is out of line), then the first step in correcting the tendency is to see it for what it is: a habit. A habit is a pattern of behavior woven into seeming permanence by repetition. If I repeatedly and consistently put off doing the tough tasks in favor of the easy ones, it will become a habit. It's the law of the human neurological system.

So, what do we do? We build a new habit to create a routine. That's right, a routine! Please repeat to yourself, "I don't need self-discipline for this, I don't need a new personality, I don't need fresh strength of character or even more willpower: *All I need is a routine.*"

One of our top mentors and business productivity coaches, Lyndon Duke, once said that he had spent many years lowering his self-esteem by bemoaning the condition of his messy apartment. He lived alone and was a highly active business genius who worked many long and joyful hours, but couldn't keep his place clean. He told himself that he was an undisciplined and disorganized person. Soon, in his own mind, he was a slob. Permanent characteristic: slob.

Finally it dawned on him that the only thing missing was a routine. That's all he lacked! He didn't lack willpower, good character, or self-control. He simply lacked a routine.

So he made up a routine: "I will straighten things up for 20 minutes every morning." Mondays, while coffee was brewing and eggs simmering, for just a few short and quick minutes he would do his living room. Tuesdays, his kitchen. Wednesdays, the bedroom. Thursdays, the hall and porch. Fridays, the home office and den. And each Saturday morning, for 20 minutes, we would do a deeper cleaning of his choice. That became his routine. The beauty of a routine is that it eventually becomes habit.

"At first, it was awkward and weird," he said. "And I thought to myself that it was so unnatural and uncomfortable that I would probably never follow through, but I promised myself a 90-day free trial. I'd be free to drop it if my theory was incorrect. My theory was that I only needed a routine, and that once my routine *became routine*, it would be an effortless and natural part of my life."

He was absolutely correct about all of it. When we first visited him at his place, long after his routine had become habit, we noticed how clean and orderly it looked. We assumed he had someone come in to clean. Then he told us about the power, the absolutely stunning and amazing power of making up a routine.

"I do it so naturally now that sometimes I don't even remember having done it," he said. "So I'll have to look out at my living room to check, and lo and behold, it's in complete order. I had done it without thinking."

Do you hate yourself because you don't prepare for your team meetings? Are you troubled by how your e-mail is taking up your precious time and life as a leader? You aren't missing any kind of inner strength; you are missing a routine. Check your e-mail two specific times a day and tell your people that's what you do.

If something isn't happening in your professional life, if you could be more productive if only you were "as disciplined as so and so," then worry no longer. It isn't about you. It's about your lack of a routine. All you need is a routine. Make up your routine and follow your routine, and if you do this for 90 days, it will be so effortless and natural to you that you'll never have to think about it again.

98. Deliver the Reward

Love is always creative and fear is always destructive.
If you could only love enough, you would be the most
powerful person in the world.
—Emmet Fox, author and philosopher

The most important principle of motivation is this: You get what you reward. It's true of every relationship. It's true of pets, houseplants, children, and lovers. You get what you reward. It's especially true of team motivation. Positive reinforcement of the desired behavior works much faster and much more permanently than criticizing poor behavior. Love conquers fear every time. Leaders who figure out, on their own, ways to reward their people for good performance get more good performances than leaders who run around all day putting out fires caused by their people's poor performance.

The reason most people don't maximize this reward concept is that they wait too long to put it into effect. They wait to decide whether to reward people, and soon, before they know it, a big problem comes up to be dealt with. By then it's too late.

Dedicate a certain portion of each day to rewarding people, even if it's only a verbal reward. Get on the phone. Send out some e-mails. Reward. Reward. Sometimes verbal and written rewards, rather than financial bonuses and prizes, are the ones that go the farthest in inspiring a person to do more.

Obtain a copy of Bob Nelson's *1001 Ways to Reward Employees*, an excellent study of how companies reward their people, and read it with a yellow highlighter or a red pen in hand. Those who do this increase their team's productivity. Those who do this underline and highlight completely different parts of the book and then translate the ideas into ideas to fit their style. Most of the ideas don't take any extra time, just extra commitment to reward.

99. Slow Down

Nothing so conclusively proves a man's ability to lead others as what he does from day to day to lead himself.
—Thomas J. Watson,
Former CEO, IBM

You'll lead better if you slow down. You'll get more done, too. It doesn't seem as though it would be true. It doesn't seem as though slowing down would get that much more done. But it does. Every day you do it, you will get more done. Every day you experiment with slowing down, you will understand the truth behind the legend of the tortoise and the hare.

The most important element of slowing down is to know that you're always working on the right thing at any given time. Business consultant Chet Holmes says that he and his clients accomplish this by making sure each day has only six things on the must-do list. That list lets them slow down.

"Why only six things?" says Holmes. "Because with a bigger list than that, generally you just try to trim the list. You spend the day trimming the list. At the end of the day you feel that most of the important things on the list did not get completed. You just look down and say, 'Oh, I didn't do the most important things.' There's a bad psychological impact in not finishing your list! And so only list the six most important things…and then *make sure* you get them done. You'll be amazed at how much you've accomplished."

If I am on the wrong road, it doesn't matter how good I get at speeding down the road. It's still the wrong road. I need to remind myself of this: Slow down and win. I need to take my sweet, gentle time. I want this conversation ahead of me to be relaxed and strong so that the relationship I have becomes relaxed and strong. So all day, it helps to tell myself: Slow down. Even slower than that.

100. Decide to Be Great

When life demands more of people than they demand of life—as is ordinarily the case—what results is a resentment of life almost as deep-seated as the fear of death. —Tom Robbins, author

Either now or on your deathbed, you'll realize a strange truth: There's no excuse for not being great. If you are a leader, a leader it is what you are. If you are still just a manager, just managing to manage, well, maybe you'll manage, but how fulfilling is that? How proud is your subconscious mind of you? How proud is your family?

Someday you will just decide to be *great* at what you do. You'll never look back. You'll never regret the decision. It might not have seemed like a big deal at the moment you decided, but somehow you'll know the decision is final. It will not have to be revisited. There's a reason why it's good to be great: People want to follow you. People start to respect you. People want to be more like you. People want to do things for you.

And if you are honest with yourself, you will someday realize the truth for yourself, either now, or on your deathbed: There was no excuse for not being great.

101. Show Your People the "Want to"

He who has a why can endure any how.
—Friedrich Nietzsche

Effective leaders learn to grasp a key distinction—a contrast between two ideas. The first idea is the "how to" and the second idea is the "want to." Most of the people you are trying to motivate believe that what's missing in their lives is the "how to." When they come to you for coaching, they often say, "I *want* to achieve this, but I don't know *how* to do it. I *want* to succeed at this, but I don't know *how*."

What they believe is missing is the "how to." What's really missing, however, is the "want to"—the desire, the focus, the commitment, the willingness to devote time—focused, uninterruptable time toward that thing that they say they don't know *how* to do, because the "how to" is always everywhere.

The beautiful thing about living in the age we live in is that the Internet is everywhere and we can find anything online—how to do this, how to do that, how to write a great sales e-mail, how to research a customer's company. So, the "how to" is not really missing.

What's missing is the time warrior in you who carves out, with a sword, devoted, dedicated, uninterruptable time for what it is you want to achieve.

That's the secret formula that people do not follow. We call that the "want to." When we can increase the "want to," it always shows up as time devoted. If I *want to* paint my house, it will show up as time blocked out for painting my house. It's a really simple formula. If I *want* to write a book, it shows up on my calendar as time blocked out for writing my book. If I *want* to have a better relationship with my team, that shows up as time blocked out to be with them and listen to them.

102. Learn to Encourage Testing

The biggest job we have is to teach a newly hired employee how to fail intelligently. We have to train him to experiment over and over and to keep on trying and failing until he learns what will work.
—Charles Kettering

How do we teach our people to access their "want to"? How do they put time in the calendar? That's the most important part of achieving anything. So that's what motivating others is about. It's about two very curious opposing ideas that most people have connected, called *testing* versus *trusting*. Most people believe that those two things are intertwined—I need to trust something before I test it. I need to trust that this will work before I give it a fair test. But when your people learn to drop the trust part of that equation, they accomplish things so much faster and they really have fun in life.

Allow your people to experience how much fun it is to test what life would be like if they dropped the trusting part and just started testing things. After you suggest a new course of action, your team members will often tell you something that keeps them from getting the effective professional the life they want. They will say, "Well, I guess I just have to trust that the method that you recommended for doing this will work—I guess I'll just have to trust that that would work for *me*. I guess I would just have to trust it—I'll have to trust it."

Then you might say, "No, please, don't trust it."

Their belief that you have to trust something, is really poor time management because they are adding a task to their to-do list that they don't need to add, and a difficult, complex task at that—trusting! Trusting ahead of time that something will work that they have no experience of. How do they do that? Don't ask them to. Ask them to merely test it. They don't need to figure out how to trust something before they move on to the testing phase.

Most people stop themselves. They think, *I don't believe it would work. I don't have enough desire for it. I don't have enough passion. I don't trust it yet. I guess I have to be more of a believer before I start this program.*

And so they are all hung up on all these very sentimental, emotional ideas. What stops them from succeeding is sentimentality. Sentimentality shows up in things such as believing in yourself, believing in a process, trusting this, wishing, hoping, confidence—all these romantic concepts that stop us. We believe they're necessary—"I guess I really have to believe in myself in order to move forward and be a good salesperson." Not at all! Just test the principles. Test our sales system.

When you were a baby you didn't have to trust that walking would work. You didn't have to think if you were to learn to walk the way grown-ups walked; you had to trust the process.

You stumbled around, you staggered around, and you fell and you giggled, or you fell and you cried. But then you got back up and you stumbled a while more and finally you were walking. There wasn't really a trust factor in there that you had to master first. You were a baby. You were adventurous. You had a willingness to test.

As you got older you saw that your friends were riding bikes in the neighborhood and your brother and sister had a bike and they all rode easily and happily. But the more you looked at a bicycle, the more you saw that it didn't seem to make sense that these two wheels would hold you up. It sure looked like you would just tip over if you got on the bike. So you would get up on the bike and fall over. But then you finally stayed up. You never had to trust that the bicycle would hold you up in order to ride it; all you had to do was be willing to test it.

This is always true of leadership and motivating others. When systems are introduced to you by your own leaders, you lead the way by your willingness to jump in and test them. When you pass down new systems, you ask for the same thing: testing.

In today's world, the technology changes constantly. We encounter more change in a year than our parents did in a lifetime. There is huge resistance to change and great skepticism about new systems. When you embrace the value of testing, you stop wasting time trying to trust things and asking your people to trust you or the organization. Don't worry when your people don't believe something will work. You are not asking that.

Remember that when you learned to ride a bike, you didn't trust it at all. Maybe your self-talk was, *This will never work.*

I don't see how this could work. It might work for others, but I don't think it will work for me. When your people voice those thoughts, let them know that those thoughts are fine. Most managers think if their people think that about their sales process, or about the new system for communicating by text with customers, they have to change everyone's feelings up front. Not true.

The child gets back on the bike because the child is simply testing. Not trusting. Not even caring about trusting, but testing, testing, testing, testing, until "Look at me, I'm riding!" Our recommendation when people learn a new "how to" is to test it—over and over—instead of trying to figure out how to trust it. Steve has a coaching school that teaches principles and practices for building a prosperous business. And inside the school, he's got two very powerful faculty members who have the systems, methods, and strategies for getting clients which are proven to work, are beautifully taught, and which, when practiced, really do work for people.

There is no trusting involved. Yet people prior to coming to the school read up on these strategies and options and systems for building their practice and they say, "I guess I'm just going to have to trust that coming to this school will work for me."

And Steve says, "You know, you don't. I'll tell you what the experience is of people who have been to the school. Those who practice (test) the disciplines in the school, succeed. And you can come practice and test; or you can come, bite your nails, and wonder if this will work for you. But if you are all about trusting and observing versus jumping in, then it will be like going to the gym and pulling up a lawn chair and watching everyone work out. You'll be learn all about working out without testing and going in there and trying stuff. It's the *action* that moves people forward; it is not learning to trust that that action would move you forward."

The most exciting breakthroughs in selling have occurred when clients and customers are allowed to *test* products and services before buying. Some people refer to this breakthrough as "content selling," but it's really a simple respect for testing as the most powerful way to get someone to buy.

We often call it the puppy dog sales system. If you go into a pet shop looking to buy a dog and you can't decide, and the salesperson says, "Tell you what. Just take that little puppy you were holding home for a couple days. No charge. No obligation. If you don't want to buy him, bring him back to us." That's testing at its best, and you can do that everywhere.

103. Teach the Love of Challenge

Life is a challenge, meet it. —Mother Theresa

Some of the biggest breakthroughs in the lives of leaders we work with have come from seeing the benefits of challenge. We've seen how it helps us, too, to challenge ourselves, and it helps us to look upon things that we saw previously as problems and see them now now as challenges that benefit us. And when we can see it that way, when we can really embrace the benefit of challenge, then we can have a completely different life leading others than most managers have.

Most managers avoid challenges, and when they can't avoid them, they get upset over them. This leads to low personal morale in the manager and very low morale on the team watching the manager struggle with fresh challenges. Most managers, especially those in the victim mindset, have this kind of work life: They wake up in the morning and they try to figure out what they are going to avoid. They wake up and they say, "Oh, my gosh, what do I dread? Let me look at my calendar. What do I have to do? What are my obligations? What do I hope does not happen?"

This is a life that is being lived with a subconscious mission to avoid challenge. Because this person doesn't see the benefit of challenge, he sees challenge as an affront and insult to the comfortable life; and so he tries to avoid it and he ends up being *more* challenged than other people, in the long run, because he hasn't seen the value of the "obstacle."

Let's look at a physical example of the benefits of challenge. Studies have shown (and we refer you to the book, *Biomarkers*, but you can check this out for yourself with your own body) that people who challenge themselves physically end up feeling better—having a better life, having more energy, having more clarity, having more spirit.

They did studies with people in their 80s and 90s and gently they began bringing weights in. What a horrible thing— poor 85 year old—you are going to make him lift weights? Are you kidding? What happened was these people got stronger. Their hearts got better, their health got better, their outlook got better, their lung capacity improved. Their metabolism was better, their nervous system was better, the circulation in their bodies really got better from lifting weights—at the age of 85, at the age of 90. So this is the benefit of challenge. Challenge the body!

A lot of times you as a leader will have a person report to you challenged by some "problem" (and we are putting the word "problem" in quotes) and she's so upset that she has to deal with the problem, not seeing that dealing with this problem is going to make her happier, stronger, and better as a professional. She doesn't see the benefit of the challenge. Motivating others well includes allowing them to warm up to challenges in life and not automatically back away. It grows your people. If they could start seeing the benefit of challenge, life would get to be so much more fun and they would be stronger.

The way to see the benefit of challenge is not to sit and repeat affirmations in the morning—"Challenges benefit me... challenges benefit me." That could be a good start, but follow it up with experimentation and *see* if challenges benefit you. And the way to do that is to challenge yourself as a leader.

You're about to launch a work project. How would you like to challenge yourself? Where do you want to push yourself? What new ground would you like to break? As you do this, let your people observe you. Being the role model for this is 100 times more effective as a teaching tool than actually teaching it.

We were working with a very creative person who is a client of ours, and we were doing a session over Skype, and he was beaming. His life had taken off, he was serving so many people, and he was a very happy person. He looked into the camera on Skype, and he said, "This recession is the best thing that's ever happened to this country."

The reason he could say that was because of how he valued challenge. Valuing challenge is what gets you the life that you envisioned when you were younger. When you were a kid and you said, "Hey, let's see if we can jump off this!" We knew intuitively that's where the fun was. That's where the real fun was—in challenges, not in comfort. If you walked up to a really energetic child and said, "I know you are playing and you're running and you're jumping off this and you're crashing your bike and it looks really dangerous so I want to give you comfort instead. Come on into the house, we're going to give you a lot of chocolate and food and put on a DVD, sweetheart. We're going to give you some comfort."

A child would say, "Later!"

An adult would take you up on it.

Parents often project their own misguided need for comfort onto their children, and so do leaders onto their people. But this comfort thing is misguided. It's a mistake.

Our country is still going through a seemingly end-less recession. It is going through a wonderfully challenging time because credit cards have been taken away from people—"Sorry, no more free money" and other things are being taken away—"Oops, housing isn't free, we just said it was," and even jobs have been taken away.

People don't automatically want challenge. They want comfort. They want retirement. They want absolutely no work. And it is insane because the unchallenged life is miserable. People talk excitedly about the challenges they faced. People talk about what they went up against.

Dr. Thomas Szasz put it best when he observed, "Every act of conscious learning requires the willingness to suffer an injury to one's self-esteem. That is why young children, before they are aware of their own self-importance, learn so easily."

104. Learn How to Help a Pessimist

Pessimism leads to weakness, optimism to power.

—William James

Throughout the years when we have coached people or gone into organizations and trained people, we have found that the fastest way to convert someone from being a pessimist to being a optimist is through inspiration. Victims and pessimists hate to be fixed, hate to be corrected, and even hate to be taught things, because their whole position is defensive.

When managers have team members with victim mindsets, they often make the mistake of trying to correct it by making it wrong. They may say, "Well, you know you are kind of a victim—you are very pessimistic about this project," and the person then becomes even more defensive and will then try to defend his position in such a way that it becomes a more entrenched position! Now it's even harder to move him off the pessimistic position because he has felt the need to defend it. He felt threatened by your accusation.

Even though your intention was to have him become a happier person and have the bigger outlook, what you've really done is push him deeper into his own pessimism by trying to fix and correct him.

Many people make this mistake, and not just in business, either. They criticize their teenage son for being moody and pessimistic and it only drives that poor young person deeper into that position because all he can hear is *there's something wrong with me, you don't approve of me, you don't understand me.* Now there is even greater alienation.

All this fixing, correcting, improving, and criticizing does not motivate others. It is not strong or effective leadership. It will not help a pessimist to identify herself as a pessimist, or show her improved or better ways to think of things. It will not work and it will not help.

The fastest, best way to help a pessimist is through something called inspiration. *Have I become an inspirational figure in this person's life?* That's the most useful inner inquiry.

People often say, "I have a real victim in my life. I have tried to help her over and over, I've tried to show her the light and she won't do it and she has become even more of a victim."

We ask, "Are you a figure of inspiration in her life? Do you represent something inspiring to her? Because if you don't, you will not help her." And so, once again, the real work is not on these people in my life, the real work is on me. Motivating others always begins with me.

Could I become more of an inspirational figure? If I'm not an inspirational figure in the lives of these pessimists around me, they will not convert to optimism through me. They may convert to optimism through some inspiring event, person, or situation (even an inspiring book can get it going), but it won't be through me unless I have become an inspiring figure in their lives. That's the route to conversion from being a victim into being an owner, from being a pessimist into being an optimist—it happens through inspiration.

Look back on your own life. All the major changes you have made that have moved you toward the light—toward greater creativity, toward more courage, toward better leadership, toward more maturity and effectiveness. They always occur through inspiration. They never occur through somebody criticizing you, fixing you, making you wrong, hurting your feelings, or making you defensive. That is not an effective route to change. It will not change another person.

A lot of people say, "Well, what about constructive criticism? What about honest critical feedback?" Well, really, there's no such thing as constructive criticism. Look back throughout your life. Notice how something or someone *inspiring* shows up and then boom, you go up the ladder to a higher level of being awake, conscious, creative, and courageous.

On the other hand, look back on your life and ask yourself whether any criticism from parents, family, or people you've worked with has ever been constructive? We don't mean whether you have ever benefited from it or if you found a way after the emotions went away to listen to and use it. We are asking how constructive it was in the moment. Did it construct something? Did you build upon it right there on the spot, or did you get defensive? Did you go deeper into justifying whatever it was you were being criticized for? Constructive criticism is really the most misguided idea in the whole world of business, relationhips, parenting, team-building, and motivating other people.

105. Switch to Enthusiasm

> A mediocre idea that generates enthusiasm will go
> further than a great idea that inspires no one.
> —Mary Kay Ash

So what works? Inspiration. Enthusiasm. Generating love for the mission. This change has to occur in someone's life. How do I have my pessimist experience that? I can't control that person. My only shot is through being a model and example of inspiration—someone who inspires that person by how I listen, how I communicate, who I am. When that becomes inspirational, change happens. If I am leading a team of people I want to *be* who I want them to be. Not just say who I want them to be. I want to show them what that's like.

If they see me with a customer or a prospect, I want to demonstrate what it's like to love the customer, or to sell to the prospect in such a way that an agreement is created and a deal is done quickly. I want to show them and inspire them.

People watch the Olympics, and gym memberships increase. Every time. They are inspired by what they see. They are inspired by who other people are being. Or they see someone sing on YouTube and it goes all around the Internet and everybody gets tears in their eyes. Voice lessons increase all around town.

When people do great things, and we observe it, it makes us want to go do the same thing. So the route to helping anybody—a pessimist, a victim, anybody—is by working on myself and having my world be more inspiring for people, by having the way I live and interact with them be something that inspires enthusiasm and love. When they feel the love, that's what gives people a chance at change. People want to see it. They don't want to hear what's wrong. They want to see what's right.

106. See Your People as Perfect

Find the best in everybody. Wait long enough, and people will surprise and impress you. It might even take years, but people will show you their good side. Just keep waiting. —Randy Pausch

Here's the final paradox in helping a pessimist or a victim: People change faster when they don't need to. If I'm sitting with you and in my eyes and in my heart you're perfect the way you are, you now have more freedom to change. You now have a sense of safety and peace and openness to change.

If my wife walks in and says, "I think I'm going to go on a diet," And I say, "Thank goodness!" that's not going to go over well. I may say I'm only being supportive, but you know it's headed south. What would be the best thing I could say? She says she's going on a diet, and I say: "Why?"

"Well, don't you think I should lose some weight?"

"No, I think you're perfect the way you are. I don't have any opinion on that. That's your business, your world, it's your life. I'm fine with you. You're the perfect you for me."

"Well, okay. So you don't think I should lose weight?"

"Not if you don't want to."

"Well, I do want to."

"Well, then you should because I want you to have what you want."

"Will you support me? Will you help me? Will you help me fix the dishes I'm going to be eating on this program?"

"Of course."

"Because you think I should lose weight, don't you?"

"No. It's just some project you're on. You love it, so I'm into it."

"All right, then."

You can do that same thing to motivate people. The wife is now even *more* motivated than if she felt criticized or judged. If someone is perfect the way he is, he has freedom now to create a new path without feeling he needs to, he has to, or that he *should* because of other people's judgments.

Beliefs about other people's opinions of me are poor motivators. All those beliefs will not allow it to happen. Those beliefs will have you *not* do something, thinking you *should*. But thinking it would be cool, fun, and that you would love it—now we're talking motivation!

I want to live optimism. I don't want to preach it. So many people make that mistake. "I try to tell my children... I've always tried to teach them how to... I try to get them to be more...." Let them see it. Even the tone of your voice was not optimistic. You're really upset. You're really upset with them for not being optimists. *You* are the victim. You are the pessimist in this—not them. They are just being themselves. So, relax. Work on yourself, let life happen, watch what occurs with the pessimists, and be okay if it's nothing right away. Let them be perfect first.

107. Learn to Master Problem-Solving

Every problem has a gift for you in its hands.
—Richard Bach

What happens when problems come up? What can we do to solve these problems quickly?

Step one when a problem comes up is to **capture your problem.**

Write it down. Take it away from the emotional realm, from the ephemeral realm of something horrible, a sense of doom, a terrible feeling. To take it out of that realm, write it down, and put it somewhere where you can see it. This reduces the problem to writing. You know the phrase, "Can we reduce this to writing?" You think the key word in that phrase is *writing* but it's actually *reduce*! Your problem is immediately reduced.

Whenever my problem is being carried in my head, there is unfinished business and that will always stand between me and whatever I'm doing. I won't really do what I'm doing in a fully self-expressive way when I have this problem in my head and it isn't being managed. It isn't being captured, it hasn't been put down.

Step two is—**redefine the problem.**

We don't just mean some kind of papering over, here, with some false new word. We mean really, truly convert this thing (whatever it is) from a problem into a project.

I'm actually glad to have projects in front of me that I can work on. I derive my professional self-esteem, my sense of accomplishment, my sense of fulfillment, my inner pride, from finishing projects. The truth about problems is that problems are actually good for us, especially if we don't think of them as problems. So we want to quickly take that negative emotional charge out of the word and redefine it as a project.

Step three is **get help!**

In other words, go to someone. Sit down with your accountant. If you have a coach, sit down with your coach. Take the project that you've written out and put it in front of your coach or mentor or coworker and look at it together.

The good thing about having a coach, a consultant, or anybody who can work with you is that that other person is not going to bring any emotional baggage to the project whatsoever. That other person is going to have great distance from the situation. We human beings love trying to solve things.

The real trouble comes in when we think these things we are trying to solve shouldn't be in our lives. When you've got someone sitting across from you who doesn't have the emotional connection you do to the situation, she can see so many possibilities and so many options.

Now we get to step four, the most important step in solving a problem. This is the one you always want to make sure you do, but this is the step in problem-solving that people really don't want to do.

Step four is **complete your project.**

One of the last pieces of the puzzle of how to really be productive and prolific and successful in life—is to see the value in *completing* things. Notice how much energy it takes to hold all kinds of unfinished business in your mind. In fact, it takes more energy to carry around unfinished business than it does to complete everything on your list—a lot more.

Try it someday. Just do things without considering whether you feel like doing them, and do everything you can think of that's unfinished. Notice at the end of that day how much *energy* you've got! That's the real paradox: when you finish something, your sense of energy about life, your clarity, and your joy in living goes up—it doesn't go down from having worked on something.

If you notice at the end of a football game, the team that wins is jumping all over the field. Where do they get the energy? They have just been playing their hearts out all night long and here they are leaping and jumping into each other's arms and running in circles and running around and around the field. Now they go into the locker room and they're yelling and whooping, and then they go out and party all night long. A victory on the field feels complete. We completed what we set out to do. There's no unfinished business here.

Now you notice the team on the other side and they're just wiped out. They need help to get to the locker room. They're completely exhausted and they go home and they are collapsing. The reason they're wiped out is that their work feels so unfinished. All these unfinished things in my life are pulling at me. They're robbing me. They're like mind parasites, and if I would just complete these things it would be a fresh new day for me and everything would look brilliant and exciting. Procrastinators are always worried about things, and the reason they are worried is that they know they don't have much of a mind left to deal with things. Because the mind gets eaten up by these parasites called unfinished tasks.

So the final step in solving problems is to make certain you are complete.

108. Welcome Every Circumstance

Nothing splendid has ever been achieved except by
those who dared to believe that something inside
them was superior to circumstance.
—Bruce Barton

Your job as a great leader is to welcome every circumstance.

Uninspiring, unmotivational managers actually de-motivate their people by reacting negatively to circumstances as they arise. The first thing I want to realize in welcoming every circumstance is the difference between perception and circumstance. There is a huge difference. Perception is what drives human behavior.

Let's say you are afraid of snakes. You don't like snakes, you think snakes are creepy, and you believe they are dangerous to you, so you don't care for them at all. You don't want one in your home. One day, you notice a snake has entered your home.

Look at how you behave. Look at your actions and thoughts. You panic, scramble, crawl out the window, call 911, call animal control, yell, and feel your heart pounding. There are all kinds of behaviors here that we could record on video as a textbook illustration of one definite way of behaving when a snake enters someone's home.

Now imagine that you are a biologist and you have specialized in snakes—that's what you most enjoy working with. You've studied them, you've worked with them in the laboratory, you've been on farms. Now you are sitting at home, and you notice a snake has entered your home.

Because you know about snakes, you can see that this snake is perfectly harmless. You can identify it right away. Now, when you see the snake, you actually light up. You actually think "Oh, my goodness, take a look at that, what a beautiful specimen," and because you know about snakes, you can get some kind of food, because you know what it likes. You lure it over to a little cage you keep for just this kind of occasion. The snake comes toward you, and you gather the snake up in your hands, admire it, and say, "Boy, what a beautiful specimen—what a sweet little boy this is."

Look at those two different ways of responding to a snake. Notice the circumstance here was "snake enters house." That's the circumstance. A circumstance cannot directly cause a response or an action on your part. Only a perception can do that. We have circumstances in our lives such as recession, downsizing, job loss, poor sales figures, divorce, bad weather—all kinds of circumstances occur. But how we act and feel are not because of the circumstances, but rather our perception of them.

The first person who saw the snake panicked based on his perception. The perception was that snakes are a threat. For the second person, the biologist, the perception was that snakes are fascinating and welcome.

The good news here is I can change my perception. I'm in charge of my perceptions. Circumstance has nothing to do with any of this. I can consciously change my perception of small changes in the organization or even large changes, such as a recession. I can help my people do the same thing. I may feel down about the recession, but then I can challenge my beliefs and thoughts. Maybe the great thing about a recession or anything out there that challenges complacency is that I rise up in response to it, like a kite rises against the wind. If there's no opposing wind, the kite can't fly. If there's no challenge for me, I cannot become stronger. I cannot grow. If there's no weight to lift, the arm cannot grow muscle. So this thing I'm calling a recession that I'm labeling as bad, I can choose to label as good.

Thoughts to help your perception are: *What's good about this? What's great about this? What strengthens me? What can make me better because of this?*

Perceptions drive behavior. Perceptions drive feelings. Perceptions drive thought patterns, either toward the very, very creative or back down to the self-pitying and destructive. Self-destructive thought patterns come from fearful perception. I can switch perceptions any time I want. That's the ultimate in creativity.

109. Do What's Required

Is what you are doing in the next hour highly productive for you? Is it your next necessary required action? Or are you just keeping busy? —Dusan Djukich

Of all the thousands of books on leadership and management our absolute favorite is Dusan Djukich's *Straight-Line Leadership*. In it Djukich contrasts leaders who go in circles all day with leaders who go in a straight line, from A to B, getting the results they want. His central premise is that we all know what to do to get the result we want. He asks leaders to identify the objective, and then list the *necessary required actions that must be taken*.

Notice the power in the words *necessary, required,* and *must.* There is no wiggle room. No way to get vague or bail out by confronting a host of options. Just do the necessary required action. It wakes you up.

Dusan Djukich is a powerful leadership coach who begins his work with leaders by asking pointed, straight questions. He has given us permission to share some of his questions here, so that you might ask them of yourself and the people who report to you:

- What would make this conversation amazingly useful to you?
- How do you want to use the rest of your life?
- What if you could give 100% with or without fear?
- What's missing? (I can't be useful if I don't know what's missing.)
- What would life be like if you responded differently?
- Is this useful? In what way?

- Is this too much information?
- How do you want this to go?
- What experience do you want by achieving this?
- What purpose would that serve?
- What is occurring that tells you that?
- What would it look like if it were resolved?
- Based on what you are up to, what would you like to create?
- So, what agreement do we have?

110. Transformation, Not Information

To bankrupt a fool, give him information.
—Nassim Nicholas Taleb

The final way to motivate others is to use the books and mentors and leadership training that motivates you as transformation, not information. Take the parts of the book that you have highlighted and use them out there in the game of real life. Think in terms of *tools, not rules.*

You already have a lot of information. The key to becoming masterful at motivating others is to turn your information into transformation—real change. Choose something and practice it. Pick a passage and put it to use. Turn the book into a workbook. Make it a playbook, not a book of theories. Take action based on the book.

Information will slow you down. But transformation will speed you up. Rather than seeing a book as a bunch of good ideas, turn the whole book into an action plan. Partner with someone in holding each other accountable for learning the lessons in the book and putting them to use.

When leaders receive this book as a part of the seminars we give on motivating others, they often ask, "How do you think this book will help me? What do you think I should do with it?" Our answer is always the same: "Follow the simple directions."

You can read an instruction manual on riding a bike and then walk away with that information added to your already-crowded brain. Or, you could read the manual, set the book down, and *get on the bike.*

Bibliography

Bennis, Warren. *On Becoming a Leader*, Revised Edition. Philadelphia, Penn.: Perseus Publishing, 2009.

Branden, Nathaniel. *Self Esteem at Wor: How Cofnfident People Make Powerful Companies*. New York: Jossey-Bass, 1998.

Collins, Jim. *Good to Great: Why Some Companies Make the Leap and Others Don't*. New York: HarperBusiness, 2001.

Coonradt, Charles. *The Game of Work: How to Enjoy Work as Much as Play*. Layton, Utah: Gibbs Smith, 2007.

Dauten, Dale. *The Laughing Warriors: How to Enjoy Killing the Status Quo*. Self-published. Lumina Media, 2003.

Djukich, Dusan. *Straight-Line Leadership: Tools for Living With Velocity and Power in Turbulent Times*. Bandon, Ore.: Robert Reed Publishers, 2011.

Goss, Tracy. *The Last Word on Power: Executive Reinvention for Leaders Who Must Make the Impossible Happen*. New York: Crown Business, 1995.

Hill, Napoleon. *Think and Grow Rich*, Revised Edition. New York: Tribeca Books, 2012.

Nelson, Bob. *1001 Ways to Reward Employees*, 2nd Edition. New York: Workman Publishing Company, 2005.

Taleb, Nassim Nicholas. *The Black Swan: The Impact of the Highly Improbable*. New York: Random House, 2007.

Index

About the Authors

Steve Chandler is a keynote speaker and corporate leadership coach with a large number of Fortune 500 clients. He is also a popular convention speaker (Arthur Morey of Renaissance Media said, "Steve Chandler is the most original and inspiring figure in the highly competitive field of motivational speaking.") Chandler's first book, *100 Ways to Motivate Yourself*, was named *Chicago Tribune*'s Audiobook of the Year in 1997. Chandler's books, now in seven languages, have also become best-sellers around the world. He can be reached at *www.stevechandler.com*.

Scott Richardson grew up in Detroit, Michigan, and Tucson, Arizona. He graduated in 1980 from Brigham Young University with a BA in English and a minor in Chinese. In 1983, he received a law degree from The College of Law at Arizona State University. He has practiced immigration law and injury law for more than 20 years, and has been coaching executives since 2000. This is his first of many books. He lives with his family in Arizona.

Also by Steve Chandler

100 Ways to Motivate Yourself
Reinventing Yourself
50 Ways to Create Great Relationships
The Joy of Selling
17 Lies that are Holding You Back
RelationShift

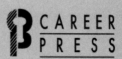